Beyond Culture

THE WORKS OF LIONEL TRILLING

UNIFORM EDITION

LIONEL TRILLING

BEYOND CULTURE

Essays on Literature and Learning

A HARVEST / HBJ BOOK

HARCOURT BRACE JOVANOVICH

NEW YORK AND LONDON

First published in 1965

Copyright © 1955, 1957, 1961, 1962, 1963, 1965 by Lionel Trilling

Printed in the United States of America

"Hawthorne in Our Time" was originally published (as "Our Hawthorne") in *Hawthorne Centenary Essays,* edited by Roy Harvey Pearce, Copyright © 1964 by the Ohio State University Press.

LIBRARY OF CONGRESS CATALOGING IN PUBLICATION DATA
Trilling, Lionel, 1905–1975.
Beyond culture.
(The works of Lionel Trilling)
(A Harvest/HBJ book)
Bibliography: p.
I. Title. II. Series: Trilling, Lionel, 1905–1975.
Works.
[PS3539.R56B4   1979]   809   79-11660
ISBN 0-15-611891-2

First Harvest/HBJ edition 1979

A B C D E F G H I J

To My Son James

Preface

FROM time to time the essays I have published are reproached for making use of the pronoun "we" in a way that is said to be imprecise and indiscriminate. Sometimes the objection is made with considerable irritation—the writer angrily declines to be included in the "we" that is being proposed, and denounces my presumptuousness in putting him where he does not belong. But one writer, reviewing a book of mine in the *Times Literary Supplement,* dealt with my "we" in a quiet and considerate way and inevitably his words came home to me. He said that when I spoke of what "we" think or feel it was often confusing because sometimes it meant "just the people of our time as a whole; more often still Americans in general; most often of all a very narrow class, consisting of New York intellectuals as judged by [my] own brighter students in Columbia."

This may well be an all too accurate description of my practice, although I would wish to claim for my awareness of the narrow class of New York intellectuals a rather fuller experience than is here imputed to me. For the rest, if I try to discern the range of my pronoun, I would say that it very likely does move among the entities of diverse size that the writer names. As a minor rhetorical device, employed in the effort to describe the temper of our age, it is not remarkable for its ingenuity, and I can see that it might be confusing: no doubt its implied assumption that there is a natural continuity among those groups so different in size involves me in loose and contradictory formulations.

Yet the assumption of cultural continuities is not easily put down. In the face of the chanciness of the generalizations it leads to, it insists on its interest and on its right to be tested. Between the intellectual temperament of an educated Englishman and an educated American the differences are very notable despite the common language and the easy flow of books and persons between the two countries. And if between England and America the differences are great, then how much greater are those between nations that do not have so many things in common. Yet the sense of the dissimilarities even between England and America must go along with the perception of what is similar or congruent in the cultures of the two nations, less in what they may be thought to derive from their respective pasts than in what they are in process of choosing from among the possibilities of the present. The differences are of rate or phase. The same may be said of certain of the differences among other nations. One cannot be aware of the large sub-culture (as we have learned to call it) of youth, of those characteristics that are shared by the young of many lands, without giving credence to the supposition that a world-wide continuity of culture tends to come into being and that it is possible to make predications about it.

If such predications can be made at all, even those that seem to be based on that "very narrow class" to which my fluctuating "we" has sometimes referred may have at least a tentative validity. The class of New York intellectuals is not remarkable for what it originates, and perhaps it says something about its nature that an eminent member of this class, an intelligent and eager-minded younger critic, could recently have found it possible to publish a volume of critical essays in which the sad word *sophisticated* was repeatedly used as a term of praise. Yet as a group it is busy and vivacious about ideas and, even more, about attitudes. Its assiduity constitutes an authority. The structure of our society is such that a class of this kind is bound by organic filaments to groups less culturally fluent which are susceptible to its influence. The great communications industries do not exactly rely for their content and methods upon the class of

New York intellectuals, yet journalism and television show its effects. At least one of the ways in which the theater and the cinema prosper is by suiting the taste which this "narrow class" has evolved. And between this small class and an analogous class in, say, Nigeria, there is pretty sure to be a natural understanding.

If one speaks of the tendency toward homogeneity in modern culture, one is necessarily implicated in the semantic difficulties of the word *culture*. These are notorious. Everyone is conscious of at least two meanings of the word. One of them refers to that complex of activities which includes the practice of the arts and of certain intellectual disciplines, the former being more salient than the latter. It is this meaning that we have in mind when we talk about popular culture as distinguished from "high" culture, or about a Ministry of Culture, or about the cultural attaché of an embassy.

The other meaning is much more inclusive. It comprises a people's technology, its manners and customs, its religious beliefs and organization, its systems of valuation, whether expressed or implicit. (If the people in question constitutes a highly developed modern nation, its social organization and its economy are usually excluded from the concept of culture and considered separately, although the reciprocal influence of social-economic and cultural factors are of course taken into account.) When the word is used in the second and larger sense, the extent of its reference includes a people's art and thought, but only as one element among others. The two meanings of the word, so different in their scope, permit us to say—it is a dubious privilege—that a certain culture sets a higher store by culture than does some other culture.

The title of this book is meant to propose both significations of the word. In its reference to the larger meaning, the phrase "beyond culture" can be said to make nonsense, for if all the implications of the word's definition are insisted on, it is not possible to conceive of a person standing beyond his culture. His culture has brought him into being in every respect except the physical, has given him his categories and habits of thought, his range of feeling, his idiom and tones of speech. No aberration can effect a real separation: even the forms that madness takes, let alone the way in which madness is evaluated, are controlled by the culture in which it occurs. No personal superiority can place one beyond these influences: the unique gifts of genius are understood to have been conditioned by the cultural conditions in which they developed; only in that time and place could they have appeared. Even when a person rejects his culture (as the phrase goes) and rebels against it, he does so in a culturally determined way: we identify the substance and style of his rebellion as having been provided by the culture against which it is directed.

Yet of course this total power that the strict definition of culture, in the large sense of the word, seems to claim for itself can have only a mere formal reality. The belief that it is possible to stand beyond the culture in some decisive way is commonly and easily held. In the modern world it is perhaps a necessary belief. When we turn from the large meaning of the word to the smaller, we readily see the extent to which the art and thought of the modern period assume that it is possible for at least some persons to extricate themselves from the culture into which they were born. Any historian of the literature of the modern age will take virtually for granted the adversary intention, the actually subversive intention, that characterizes modern writing—he will perceive its clear purpose of detaching the reader from the habits of thought and feeling that the larger culture imposes, of giving him a ground and a vantage point from which to judge and condemn, and perhaps revise, the culture that produced him.

What I am calling the modern period had its beginning in the latter part of the eighteenth century and its apogee in the first quarter of the twentieth century. We continue the direction it took. The former energy of origination is very much diminished, but we still do continue the direction: the conscious commitment to it is definitive of the artistic and intellectual culture of our time. It is a belief still pre-eminently honored that a primary function of art and thought is to liberate the individual from the tyranny of his culture in the environmental sense and to permit him to stand beyond it in an autonomy of perception and judgment.

But if the program of our present artistic and intellectual culture has not changed from that of forty or fifty years ago, the circumstances in which it has its existence have changed materially. In the doctrinal way its relation to the inclusive culture is pretty much what it once was; in the actual and operative way the relation is very different. The difference can be expressed quite simply, in numerical terms—there are a great many more people who adopt the adversary program than there formerly were. Between the end of the first quarter of this century and the present time there has grown up a populous group whose members take for granted the idea of the adversary culture. This group is to be described not only by its increasing size but by its increasing coherence. It is possible to think of it as a class. As such, it of course has its internal conflicts and contradictions, but also its common interests and presuppositions and a considerable efficiency of organization, even of an institutional kind.

The present position of the university in American life tells us much about this new state of affairs. Dr. Clark Kerr recently set forth his vision of the super-university he expects to come into being. His prophecy stipulates that this intellectual imperium, to which he gives the Baconian name of Ideopolis, shall provide a commodious place for what Dr. Kerr calls "pure creative effort," that is to say, the arts. There will perhaps be some people who regard this prospect with dismay. They will be moved by certain apprehensions which once commonly attended thoughts of bigness, of institutions, and of the academic, all of which were believed to be fatal to art. Their fears are surely anachronistic. No one who knows how things now really stand is afraid of the university. Dr. Kerr's prophecy is but a reasonable projection into the future of a condition already established and regarded with satisfaction by those who might be thought to be most jealous for the freedom of art and thought.

Three or four decades ago the university figured as the citadel of conservatism, even of reaction. It was known that behind what used to be called its walls and in its ivory towers reality was alternately ignored and traduced. The young man who committed himself to an academic career was understood to have announced his premature surrender. Now it is scarcely possible for him to be so intransigent that the university cannot be thought the proper field for his undertakings. Between the university and reality there now exists the happiest, most intimate relation. Nothing in life is so mundane and practical or so rarefied and strange that the university will not take it into sympathetic consideration.

In two of the essays of this volume I have referred to Mr. Harold Rosenberg's account of one of the conditions in which our taste in painting nowadays exists, that is, under the constantly exerted influence of a very active and authoritative criticism which is able to bring about rapid and radical changes in our aesthetic views. Objects that at one moment are not to be thought of as deserving inclusion in the category of art are at another moment firmly established in the category; criticism can also reverse this process, and our most cherished works of art (Mr. Rosenberg gives as examples the paintings of Michelangelo, Vermeer, Goya, and Cézanne) can, if an "extreme ideology" so decides, be made "not art" and may even come to seem "creatures of darkness." In the process itself there is nothing very new; for about two hundred years taste has increasingly came under the control of criticism, which has made art out of what is not art and the other way around. What *is* new is the nature of the critical agent, which perhaps explains the expeditious power it is said to have—Mr. Rosenberg tells us that the making and unmaking of art is in the hands of university art departments and the agencies which derive from them, museums and professional publications.

I cite the changed character of the university as but an example, although a particularly striking one, of the new circumstances in which the adversary culture of art and thought now exists. The change has come about, we may say, through the efforts of the adversary culture itself. It has not dominated the whole of its old antagonist, the middle class, but it has detached a considerable force from the main body of the enemy and has captured its allegiance.

The situation calls for at least a little irony. Given the legend of the free creative spirit at war with the bourgeoisie, it isn't possible to be wholly grave as we note, say, the passion that contemporary wealth feels for contemporary painting. But not more than a little irony is appropriate. For how else are civilizations ever formed save by reconciliations that were once unimaginable, save by syntheses that can be read as paradoxes? It is often true that the success of a social or cultural enterprise compromises the virtues that claimed our loyalty in its heroic, hopeless beginning, but there is a kind of vulgarity in the easy assumption that this is so always and necessarily.

Yet around the adversary culture there has formed what I have called a class. If I am right in identifying it in this way, then we can say of it, as we say of any other class, that it has developed characteristic habitual responses to the stimuli of its environment. It is not without power, and we can say of it, as we can say of any other class with a degree of power, that it seeks to aggrandize and perpetuate itself. And, as with any other class, the relation it has to the autonomy of its members makes a relevant question, and the more, of course, by reason of the part that is played in the history of its ideology by the ideal of autonomy. There is reason to believe that the relation is ambiguous.

Most of the essays in this volume were written out of an awareness of this ambiguity. Some of them propose the thought that we cannot count upon the adversary culture to sustain us in such efforts toward autonomy of perception and judgment as we might be impelled to make, that an adversary culture of art and thought, when it becomes well established, shares something of the character of the larger culture to which it was—to which it still is—adversary, and that it generates its own assumptions and preconceptions, and contrives its own sanctions to protect them. The early adversary movement of European art and thought, it has been said, based itself on the question, "Is it true? Is it true for me?" The characteristic question of our adversary culture is, "Is it true? Is it true for us?" This a good question too, it has its particular social virtues, but it does not yield the same results as the first question, and it may even make it harder for anyone to ask the first question. The difference between the force of the two questions is suggested by the latter part of my essay on Freud. The second question is asked by the group of psychiatrists to whom I refer; it serves an unquestionably useful purpose. The first question was asked by Freud himself.

Several of the essays touch on the especial difficulty of making oneself aware of the assumptions and preconceptions of the adversary culture by reason of the dominant part that is played in it by art. My sense of this difficulty leads me to approach a view which will seem disastrous to many readers and which, indeed, rather surprises me. This is the view that art does not always tell the truth or the best kind of truth and does not always point out the right way, that it can even generate falsehood and habituate us to it, and that, on frequent occasions, it might well be subject, in the interests of autonomy, to the scrutiny of the rational intellect. The history of this faculty scarcely assures us that it is exempt from the influences of the cultures in which it has sought its development, but at the present juncture its informing purpose of standing beyond any culture, even an adversary one, may be of use.

"The world doesn't fear a new idea. It can pigeonhole any idea. But it can't pigeonhole a new experience." This statement of D. H. Lawrence's is often quoted. It is a saying that has a canonical authority in our adversary culture, and it does indeed tell us much of what that culture, in its great days, intended in the way of liberation, in the way of autonomy. By an experience Lawrence meant, of course, an experience of art, and, we may suppose, of such art as derives from an experience of life. Lawrence's saying suggests that the experience speaks, as no idea ever can, to the full actuality of the person who exposes himself to it, requiring him to respond in an active way; by that response he is confirmed in his sense of personal being and its powers, and in the possibility of autonomy. If Lawrence's statement is true, surely its truth pertains to a situation in which the artist is alone and in which his audience is small and made up of isolate individuals. It has much less truth now that we are organized for the reception and accommodation of new experiences. Thus, in the process of making and unmaking art that Mr. Rosenberg describes, it is plain that experiences of painting, even of a very intense kind, submit quite docilely to being pigeonholed. Every group that organizes itself around an experience constitutes an effective pigeonhole, with the result that the demarcation between experience and idea that Lawrence took for granted as clear and certain is now hard to discern. In our adversary culture such experience as is represented in and proposed by art moves toward becoming an idea, even an ideology, as witness the present ideational and ideological status of sex, violence, madness, and art itself. If in this situation the rational intellect comes into play, it may be found that it works in the interests of experience.

L.T.

1965

Contents

Beyond Culture

On the Teaching of Modern Literature

I PROPOSE to consider here a particular theme of modern literature which appears so frequently and with so much authority that it may be said to constitute one of the shaping and controlling ideas of our epoch. I can identify it by calling it the disenchantment of our culture with culture itself—it seems to me that the characteristic element of modern literature, or at least of the most highly developed modern literature, is the bitter line of hostility to civilization which runs through it. It happens that my present awareness of this theme is involved in a personal experience, and I am impelled to speak of it not abstractly but with the husks of the experience clinging untidily to it. I shall go so far in doing this as to describe the actual circumstances in which the experience took place. These circumstances are pedagogic—they consist of some problems in teaching modern literature to undergraduates and my attempt to solve these problems. I know that pedagogy is a depressing subject to all persons of sensibility, and yet I shall not apologize for touching upon it because the emphasis upon the teaching of literature and especially of modern literature is in itself one of the most salient and significant manifestations of the culture of our time. Indeed, if, having in mind Matthew Arnold's lecture, "On the Modern Element in Literature," we are on the hunt for *the* modern element in modern literature, we might want to find it in the susceptibility of modern literature to being made into an academic subject.

For some years I have taught the course in modern literature in Columbia College. I did not undertake it without misgiving and I have never taught it with an undivided mind. My doubts do not refer to the value of the literature itself, only to the educational propriety of its being studied in college. These doubts persist even though I wholly understand that the relation of our collegiate education to modernity is no longer an open question. The unargued assumption of most curriculums is that the real subject of all study is the modern world; that the justification of all study is its immediate and presumably practical relevance to modernity; that the true purpose of all study is to lead the younge person to be at home in, and in control of, the modern world. There is really no way of quarreling with the assumption or with what follows upon it, the instituting of courses of which the substance is chiefly contemporary or at least makes ultimate reference to what is contemporary.

It might be asked why anyone should *want* to quarrel with the assumption. To that question I can return only a defensive, eccentric, self-depreciatory answer. It is this: that to some of us who teach and who think of our students as the creators of the intellectual life of the future, there comes a kind of despair. It does not come because our students fail to respond to ideas, rather because they respond to ideas with a happy vagueness, a delighted glibness, a joyous sense of power in the use of received or receivable generalizations, a grateful wonder at how easy it is to formulate and judge, at how little resistance language offers to their intentions. When that despair strikes us, we are tempted to give up the usual and accredited ways of evaluating education, and instead of prizing responsiveness and aptitude, to set store by some sign of personal character in our students, some token of individual will. We think of this as taking the form of resistance and imperviousness, of personal density or gravity, of some power of supposing that ideas are real, a power which will lead a young man to say what Goethe thought was the modern thing to say, "But is this really true—is it true for *me?*" And to say this not in the facile way, not following the progressive educational prescription to "think for yourself," which means to think in the progressive pieties rather than in the conservative pieties (if any of the latter do still exist), but to say it from his sense of himself as a person rather than as a bundle of attitudes and responses which are all alert to please the teacher and the progressive community.

We can't do anything about the quality of personal being of our students, but we are led to think about the cultural analogue of a personal character that is grave, dense, and resistant—we are led to think about the past. Perhaps the protagonist of Thomas Mann's story, "Disorder and Early Sorrow" comes to mind, that sad Professor Cornelius with his intense and ambivalent sense of history. For Professor Cornelius, who is a historian, the past is dead, is death itself, but for that very reason it is the source of order, value, piety, and even love. If we think about education in the dark light of the despair I have described, we wonder if perhaps there is not to be found in the past that quiet place at which a young man might stand for a few years, at least a little beyond the competing attitudes and generalizations of the present, at least a little beyond the contemporary problems which he is told he can master only by means of attitudes and generalizations, that quiet place in which he can be silent, in which he can *know* something—in what year the Parthenon was begun, the order of battle at Trafalgar, how Linear B was deciphered: almost anything at all that has nothing to do with the talkative and attitudinizing present, anything at all but variations on the accepted formulations about *anxiety,* and *urban society,* and *alienation,* and *Gemeinschaft* and *Gesellschaft,* all the matter of the academic disciplines which are founded upon the modern self-consciousness and the modern self-pity. The modern self-pity is certainly not without its justification; but, if the circumstances that engender it are ever to be overcome, we must sometimes wonder whether this work can be done by minds which are taught in youth to accept these sad conditions of ours as the only right objects of contemplation. And quite apart from any practical consequences, one thinks of the simple aesthetic personal pleasure of having to do with young minds, and maturing minds, which are free of cant, which are, to quote an old poet, "fierce, moody, patient, venturous, modest, shy."

This line of argument I have called eccentric and maybe it ought to be called obscurantist and reactionary. Whatever it is called, it is not likely to impress a Committee on the Curriculum. It was, I think, more or less the line of argument of my department in Columbia College, when, up to a few years ago, it would decide, whenever the question came up, not to carry its courses beyond the late nineteenth century. But our rationale could not stand against the representations which a group of students made to our Dean and which he communicated to us. The students wanted a course in modern literature—very likely, in the way of students, they said that it was a scandal that no such course was being offered in the College. There was no argument that could stand against this expressed desire: we could only capitulate, and then, with pretty good grace, muster the arguments that justified our doing so. Was not the twentieth century more than half over? Was it not nearly fifty years since Eliot wrote "Portrait of a Lady"? George Meredith had not died until 1909, and even the oldest among us had read one of his novels in a college course—many American universities had been quick to bring into their purview the literature of the later nineteenth century, and even the early twentieth century; there was a strong supporting tradition for our capitulation. Had not Yeats been Matthew Arnold's contemporary for twenty-three years?

Our resistance to the idea of the course had never been based on an adverse judgment of the literature itself. We are a department not only of English but of comparative literature, and if the whole of modern literature is surveyed, it could be said—and we were willing to say it—that no literature of the past surpassed the literature of our time in power and magnificence. Then too, it is a difficult literature, and it is difficult not merely as defenders of modern poetry say that all literature is difficult. We nowadays believe that Keats is a very difficult poet, but his earlier readers did not. We now see the depths and subtleties of Dickens, but his contemporary readers found him as simply available as a plate of oysters on the half shell. Modern literature, however, shows its difficulties at first blush; they are literal as well as doctrinal difficulties—if our students were to know their modern literary heritage, surely they needed all the help that a teacher can give?

These made cogent reasons for our decision to establish, at long last, the course in modern literature. They also made a ground for our display of a certain mean-spirited, last-ditch vindictiveness. I recall that we said something like, "Very well, if they want the modern, let them have it—let them have it, as Henry James says, full in the face. We shall give the course, but we shall give it on the highest level, and if they think, as students do, that the modern will naturally meet them in a genial way, let them have their gay and easy time with Yeats and Eliot, with Joyce and Proust and Kafka, with Lawrence, Mann, and Gide."

Eventually the course fell to me to give. I approached it with an uneasiness which has not diminished with the passage of time—it has, I think, even increased. It arises, this uneasiness, from my personal relation with the works that form the substance of the course. Almost all of them have been involved with me for a long time—I invert the natural order not out of lack of modesty but taking the cue of W. H. Auden's remark that a real book reads us. I have been read by Eliot's poems and by *Ulysses* and by *Remembrance of Things Past* and by *The Castle* for a good many years now, since early youth. Some of these books at first rejected me; I bored them. But as I grew older and they knew me better, they came to have more sympathy with me and to understand my hidden meanings. Their nature is such that our relationship has been very intimate. No literature has ever been so shockingly personal as that of our time—it asks every question that is forbidden in polite society. It asks us if we are content with our marriages, with our family lives, with our professional lives, with our friends. It is all very well for me to describe my course in the College catalogue as "paying particular attention to the role of the writer as a critic of his culture"— this is sheer evasion: the questions asked by our literature are not about our culture but about ourselves. It asks us if we are content with ourselves, if we are saved or damned—more than with anything else, our literature is concerned with salvation. No literature has ever been so intensely spiritual as ours. I do not venture to call it actually religious, but certainly it has the special intensity of concern with the spiritual life which Hegel noted when he spoke of the great modern phenomenon of the secularization of spirituality.

I do not know how other teachers deal with this extravagant personal force of modern literature, but for me it makes difficulty. Nowadays the teaching of literature inclines to a considerable technicality, but when the teacher has said all that can be said about formal matters, about verse-patterns, metrics, prose conventions, irony, tension, etc., he must confront the necessity of bearing personal testimony. He must use whatever authority he may possess to say whether or not a work is true; and if not, why not; and if so, why so. He can do this only at considerable cost to his privacy. How does one say that Lawrence is right in his great rage against the modern emotions, against the modern sense of life and ways of being, unless one speaks from the intimacies of one's own feelings, and one's own sense of life, and one's own wished-for way of being? How, except with the implication of personal judgment, does one say to students that Gide is perfectly accurate in his representation of the awful boredom and slow corruption of respectable life? Then probably one rushes in to say that this doesn't of itself justify homosexuality and the desertion of one's dying wife, certainly not. But then again, having paid one's *devoirs* to morality, how does one rescue from morality Gide's essential point about the supreme rights of the individual person, and without making it merely historical, academic?

My first response to the necessity of dealing with matters of this kind was resentment of the personal discomfort it caused me. These are subjects we usually deal with either quite unconsciously or in the privacy of our own conscious minds, and if we now and then disclose our thoughts about them, it is to friends of equal age and especial closeness. Or if we touch upon them publicly, we do so in the relative abstractness and anonymity of print. To stand up in one's own person and to speak of them in one's own voice to an audience which each year grows younger as one grows older—that is not easy, and probably it is not decent.

And then, leaving aside the personal considerations, or taking them merely as an indication of something wrong with the situation, can we not say that, when modern literature is brought into the classroom, the subject being taught is betrayed by the pedagogy of the subject? We have to ask ourselves whether in our day too much does not come within the purview of the academy. More and more, as the universities liberalize themselves, and turn their beneficent imperialistic gaze upon what is called Life Itself, the feeling grows among our educated classes that little can be experienced unless it is validated by some established intellectual discipline, with the result that experience loses much of its personal immediacy for us and becomes part of an accredited societal activity. This is not entirely true and I don't want to play the boring academic game of pretending that it *is* entirely true, that the university mind wilts and withers whatever it touches. I must believe, and I do believe, that the university study of art is capable of confronting the power of a work of art fully and courageously. I even believe that it can discover and disclose power where it has not been felt before. But the university study of art achieves this end chiefly with works of art of an older period. Time has the effect of seeming to quiet the work of art, domesticating it and making it into a classic, which is often another way of saying that it is an object of merely habitual regard. University study of the right sort can reverse this process and restore to the old work its freshness and force—can, indeed, disclose unguessed-at power. But with the works of art of our own present age, university study tends to accelerate the process by which the radical and subversive work becomes the classic work, and university study does this in the degree that it is vivacious and responsive and what is called non-academic. In one of his poems Yeats mocks the literary scholars, "the bald heads forgetful of their sins," "the old, learned, respectable bald heads," who edit the poems of the fierce and passionate young men.

> Lord, what would they say
> Did their Catullus walk this way?

Yeats, of course, is thinking of his own future fate, and no doubt there is all the radical and comical discrepancy that he sees between the poet's passions and the scholars' close-eyed concentration on the text. Yet for my part, when I think of Catullus, I am moved to praise the tact of all those old heads, from Heinsius and Bentley to Munro and Postgate, who worked on Codex G and Codex O and drew conclusions from them about the lost Codex V—for doing only this and for not trying to realize and demonstrate the true intensity and the true quality and the true cultural meaning of Catullus's passion and managing to bring it somehow into eventual accord with their respectability and baldness. Nowadays we who deal with books in universities live in fear that the World, which we imagine to be a vital, palpitating, passionate, reality-loving World, will think of us as old, respectable, and bald, and we see to it that in our dealings with Yeats (to take him as the example) his wild cry of rage and sexuality is heard by our students and quite thoroughly understood by them as—what is it that we eventually call it?—*a significant expression of our culture*. The exasperation of Lawrence and the subversiveness of Gide, by the time we have dealt with them boldly and straightforwardly, are notable instances of the *alienation of modern man as exemplified by the artist*. "Compare Yeats, Gide, Lawrence, and Eliot in the use which they make of the theme of sexuality to criticize the deficiencies of modern culture. Support your statement by specific references to the work of each author. [Time: one hour.]" And the distressing thing about our examination questions is that they are not ridiculous, they make perfectly good sense—such good sense that the young person who answers them can never again know the force and terror of what has been communicated to him by the works he is being examined on.

Very likely it was with the thought of saving myself from the necessity of speaking personally and my students from having to betray the full harsh meaning of a great literature that I first taught my course in as *literary* a way as possible. A couple of decades ago the discovery was made that a literary work is a structure of words: this doesn't seem a surprising thing to have learned except for its polemical tendency, which is to urge us to minimize the amount of attention we give to the poet's social and personal will, to what he wants to happen outside the poem as a result of the poem; it urges us to fix our minds on what is going on inside the poem. For me this polemical tendency has been of the greatest usefulness, for it has corrected my inclination to pay attention chiefly to what the poet *wants*. For two or three years I directed my efforts toward dealing with the matter of the course chiefly as structures of words, in a formal way, with due attention paid to the literal difficulty which marked so many of the works. But it went against the grain. It went against my personal grain. It went against the grain of the classroom situation, for formal analysis is best carried on by question-and-answer, which needs small groups, and the registration for the course in modern literature in any college is sure to be large. And it went against the grain of the authors themselves—structures of words they may indeed have created, but these structures were not pyramids or triumphal arches, they were manifestly contrived to be not static and commemorative but mobile and aggressive, and one does not describe a quinquereme or a howitzer or a tank without estimating how much *damage* it can do.

Eventually I had to decide that there was only one way to give the course, which was to give it without strategies and without conscious caution. It was not honorable, either to the students or to the authors, to conceal or disguise my relation to the literature, my commitment to it, my fear of it, my ambivalence toward it. The literature had to be dealt with in the terms it announced for itself. As for the students, I have never given assent to the modern saw about "teaching students, not subjects"—I have always thought it right to teach subjects, believing that if one gives his first loyalty to the subject, the student is best instructed. So I resolved to give the course with no considerations in mind except my own interests. And since my own interests lead me to see literary situations as cultural situations, and cultural situations as great elaborate fights about moral issues, and moral issues as having something to do with gratuitously chosen images of personal being, and images of personal being as having something to do with literary style, I felt free to begin with what for me was a first concern, the animus of the author, the objects of his will, the things he wants or wants to have happen.

My cultural and non-literary method led me to decide that I would begin the course with a statement of certain themes or issues that might especially engage our attention. I even went so far in non-literariness as to think that my purposes would best be served if I could contrive a "background" for the works we would read—I wanted to propose a history for the themes or issues that I hoped to discover. I did not intend that this history should be either very extensive or very precise. I wanted merely to encourage a *sense* of a history, some general intuition of a past, in students who, as it seems to me, have not been provided with any such thing by their education and who are on the whole glad to be without it. And because there is as yet no adequate general work of history of the culture of the last two hundred years, I asked myself what books of the age just preceding ours had most influenced our literature, or, since I was far less concerned with showing influence than with discerning a tendency, what older books might seem to fall into a line the direction of which pointed to our own literature and thus might serve as a prolegomenon to the course.

It was virtually inevitable that the first work that should have sprung to mind was Sir James Frazer's *The Golden Bough,* not, of course, the whole of it, but certain chapters, those that deal with Osiris, Attis, and Adonis. Anyone who thinks about modern literature in a systematic way takes for granted the great part played in it by myth, and especially by those examples of myth which tell about gods dying and being reborn—the imagination of death and rebirth, reiterated in the ancient world in innumerable variations that are yet always the same, captivated the literary mind at the very moment when, as all accounts of the modern age agree, the most massive and compelling of all the stories of resurrection had lost much of its hold upon the world.

Perhaps no book has had so decisive an effect upon modern literature as Frazer's. It was beautifully to my purpose that it had first been published ten years before the twentieth century began. Yet forty-three years later, in 1933, Frazer delivered a lecture, very eloquent, in which he bade the world be of good hope in the face of the threat to the human mind that was being offered by the Nazi power. He was still alive in 1941. Yet he had been born in 1854, three years before Matthew Arnold gave the lecture "On the Modern Element in Literature." Here, surely, was history, here was the past I wanted, beautifully connected with our present. Frazer was wholly a man of the nineteenth century, and the more so because the eighteenth century was so congenial to him—the lecture of 1933 in which he predicted the Nazi defeat had as its subject Condorcet's *Progress of the Human Mind;* when he took time from his anthropological studies to deal with literature, he prepared editions of Addison's essays and Cowper's letters. He had the old lost belief in the virtue and power of rationality. He loved and counted on order, decorum, and good sense. This great historian of the primitive imagination was in the dominant intellectual tradition of the West which, since the days of the pre-Socratics, has condemned the ways of thought that we call primitive.

It can be said of Frazer that in his conscious intention he was a perfect representative of what Arnold meant when he spoke of a modern age. And perhaps nothing could make clearer how the conditions of life and literature have changed in a hundred years than to note the difference between the way in which Arnold defines the modern element in literature and the way in which we must define it.

Arnold used the word *modern* in a wholly honorific sense. So much so that he seems to dismiss all temporal idea from the word and makes it signify certain timeless intellectual and civic virtues— his lecture, indeed, was about the modern element in the ancient literatures. A society, he said, is a modern society when it maintains a condition of repose, confidence, free activity of the mind, and the tolerance of divergent views. A society is modern when it affords sufficient material well-being for the conveniences of life and the development of taste. And, finally, a society is modern when its members are intellectually mature, by which Arnold means that they are willing to judge by reason, to observe facts in a critical spirit, and to search for the law of things. By this definition Periclean Athens is for Arnold a modern age, Elizabethan England is not; Thucydides is a modern historian, Sir Walter Raleigh is not.

I shall not go into further details of Arnold's definition or description of the modern.[1] I have said enough, I think, to suggest what Arnold was up to, what he wanted to see realized as the desideratum of his own society, what ideal he wanted the works of intellect and imagination of his own time to advance. And at what a distance his ideal of the modern puts him from our present sense of modernity, from our modern literature! To anyone conditioned by our modern literature, Arnold's ideal of order, convenience, decorum, and rationality might well seem to reduce itself to the small advan-

---

[1] I leave out of my summary account the two supreme virtues that Arnold ascribes to the most successful examples of a "modern" literature. One is the power of effecting an "intellectual deliverance," by which Arnold means leading men to comprehend the "vast multitude of facts" which make up "a copious and complex present, and behind it a copious and complex past." The other is "adequacy," the ability to represent the complex high human development of a modern age "in its completest and most harmonious" aspect, doing so with "the charm of that noble serenity which always accompanies true insight."

tages and excessive limitations of the middle-class life of a few pros-perous nations of the nineteenth century. Arnold's historic sense presented to his mind the long, bitter, bloody past of Europe, and he seized passionately upon the hope of true civilization at last achieved. But the historic sense of our literature has in mind a long excess of civilization to which may be ascribed the bitterness and bloodiness both of the past and of the present and of which the peaceful aspects are to be thought of as mainly contemptible—its order achieved at the cost of extravagant personal repression, either that of coercion or that of acquiescence; its repose otiose; its toler-ance either flaccid or capricious; its material comfort corrupt and corrupting; its taste a manifestation either of timidity or of pride; its rationality attained only at the price of energy and passion.

For the understanding of this radical change of opinion nothing is more illuminating than to be aware of the doubleness of mind of the author of *The Golden Bough*. I have said that Frazer in his con-scious mind and in his first intention exemplifies all that Arnold means by the modern. He often speaks quite harshly of the irration-ality and the orgiastic excesses of the primitive religions he describes, and even Christianity comes under his criticism both because it stands in the way of rational thought and because it can draw men away from intelligent participation in the life of society. But Frazer had more than one intention, and he had an unconscious as well as a conscious mind. If he deplores the primitive imagination, he also does not fail to show it as wonderful and beautiful. It is the rare reader of *The Golden Bough* who finds the ancient beliefs and rituals wholly alien to him. It is to be expected that Frazer's adduc-tion of the many pagan analogues to the Christian mythos will be thought by Christian readers to have an adverse effect on faith, it was undoubtedly Frazer's purpose that it should, yet many readers will feel that Frazer makes all faith and ritual indigenous to human-ity, virtually biological; they feel, as DeQuincey put it, that not to be at least a *little* superstitious is to lack generosity of mind. Scientific though his purpose was, Frazer had the effect of validating those

old modes of experiencing the world which modern men, beginning
with the Romantics, have sought to revive in order to escape from
positivism and common sense.

The direction of the imagination upon great and mysterious objects of worship is not the only means men use to liberate themselves
from the bondage of quotidian fact, and although Frazer can
scarcely be held accountable for the ever-growing modern attraction
to the extreme mental states—to rapture, ecstasy, and transcendence,
which are achieved by drugs, trance, music and dance, orgy, and the
derangement of personality—yet he did provide a bridge to the understanding and acceptance of these states, he proposed to us the
idea that the desire for them and the use of them for heuristic
purposes is a common and acceptable manifestation of human
nature.

This one element of Frazer's masterpiece could scarcely fail to
suggest the next of my prolegomenal works. It is worth remarking
that its author was in his own way as great a classical scholar as
Frazer himself—Nietzsche was Professor of Classical Philology at
the University of Basel when, at the age of twenty-seven, he published his essay *The Birth of Tragedy*. After the appearance of this
stunningly brilliant account of Greek civilization, of which Socrates
is not the hero but the villain, what can possibly be left to us of that
rational and ordered Greece, that modern, that eighteenth-century,
Athens that Arnold so entirely relied on as the standard for judging
all civilizations? Professor Kaufmann is right when he warns us
against supposing that Nietzsche exalts Dionysus over Apollo and
tells us that Nietzsche "emphasizes the Dionysiac only because he
feels that the Apollonian genius of the Greeks cannot be fully understood apart from it." But no one reading Nietzsche's essay for the
first time is likely to heed this warning. What will reach him before
due caution intervenes, before he becomes aware of the portentous
dialectic between Dionysus and Apollo, is the excitement of suddenly being liberated from Aristotle, the joy of finding himself ac-
ceding to the author's statement that "art rather than ethics consti-

tutes the essential metaphysical activity of man," that tragedy has its source in the Dionysiac rapture, "whose closest analogy is furnished by physical intoxication," and that this rapture, in which "the individual forgets himself completely," was in itself no metaphysical state but an orgiastic display of lust and cruelty, "of sexual promiscuity overriding every form of tribal law." This sadic and masochistic frenzy, Nietzsche is at pains to insist, needs the taming hand of Apollo before it can become tragedy, but it is the primal stuff of the great art, and to the modern experience of tragedy this explanation seems far more pertinent than Aristotle's, with its eagerness to forget its origin in its achievement of a state of noble imperturbability.

Of supreme importance in itself, Nietzsche's essay had for me the added pedagogic advantage of allowing me to establish a historical line back to William Blake. Nothing is more characteristic of modern literature than its discovery and canonization of the primal, non-ethical energies, and the historical point could be made the better by remarking the correspondence of thought of two men of different nations and separated from each other by a good many decades, for Nietzsche's Dionysian orgy and Blake's Hell are much the same thing.

Whether or not Joseph Conrad read either Blake or Nietzsche I do not know, but his *Heart of Darkness* follows in their line. This very great work has never lacked for the admiration it deserves, and it has been given a kind of canonical place in the legend of modern literature by Eliot's having it so clearly in mind when he wrote *The Waste Land* and his having taken from it the epigraph to "The Hollow Men." But no one, to my knowledge, has ever confronted in an explicit way its strange and terrible message of ambivalence toward the life of civilization. Consider that its protagonist, Kurtz, is a progressive and a liberal and that he is the highly respected representative of a society which would have us believe it is benign, although in fact it is vicious. Consider too that he is a practitioner of several arts, a painter, a writer, a musician, and into the bargain a political orator. He is at once the most idealistic and the most practically successful of all the agents of the Belgian exploitation of the Congo. Everybody knows the truth about him which Marlow discovers—that Kurtz's success is the result of a terrible ascendancy he has gained over the natives of his distant station, an ascendancy which is derived from his presumed magical or divine powers, that he has exercised his rule with an extreme of cruelty, that he has given himself to unnamable acts of lust. This is the world of the darker pages of *The Golden Bough*. It is one of the great points of Conrad's story that Marlow speaks of the primitive life of the jungle not as being noble or charming or even free but as being base and sordid—and for *that* reason compelling: he himself feels quite overtly its dreadful attraction. It is to this devilish baseness that Kurtz has yielded himself, and yet Marlow, although he does indeed treat him with hostile irony, does not find it possible to suppose that Kurtz is anything but a hero of the spirit. For me it is still ambiguous whether Kurtz's famous deathbed cry, "The horror! The horror!" refers to the approach of death or to his experience of savage life. Whichever it is, to Marlow the fact that Kurtz could utter this cry at the point of death, while Marlow himself, when death threatens him, can know it only as a weary grayness, marks the difference between the ordinary man and a hero of the spirit. Is this not the essence of the modern belief about the nature of the artist, the man who goes down into that hell which is the historical beginning of the human soul, a beginning not outgrown but established in humanity as we know it now, preferring the reality of this hell to the bland lies of the civilization that has overlaid it?

This idea is proposed again in the somewhat less powerful but still very moving work with which I followed *Heart of Darkness,* Thomas Mann's *Death in Venice.* I wanted this story not so much for its account of an extravagantly Apollonian personality surrendering to forces that, in his Apollonian character, he thought shameful—although this was certainly to my purpose—but rather for Aschenbach's fevered dreams of the erotic past, and in particular that dream of the goat-orgy which Mann, being the kind of writer he is, having the kind of relation to Nietzsche he had, might well have written to serve as an illustration of what *The Birth of Tragedy* means by religious frenzy, the more so, of course, because Mann chooses that particular orgiastic ritual, the killing and eating of the goat, from which tragedy is traditionally said to have been derived.

A notable element of this story in which the birth of tragedy plays an important part is that the degradation and downfall of the protagonist is not represented as tragic in the usual sense of the word—that is, it is not represented as a great deplorable event. It is a commonplace of modern literary thought that the tragic mode is not available even to the gravest and noblest of our writers. I am not sure that this is the deprivation that some people think it to be and a mark of our spiritual inferiority. But if we ask why it has come about, one reason may be that we have learned to think our way back through tragedy to the primal stuff out of which tragedy arose. If we consider the primitive forbidden ways of conduct which traditionally in tragedy lead to punishment by death, we think of them as being the path to reality and truth, to an ultimate self-realization. We have always wondered if tragedy itself may not have been saying just this in a deeply hidden way, drawing us to think of the hero's sin and death as somehow conferring justification, even salvation of a sort—no doubt this is what Nietzsche had in mind when he said that "tragedy denies ethics." What tragedy once seemed to hint, our literature now is willing to say quite explicitly. If Mann's Aschenbach dies at the height of his intellectual and artistic powers, overcome by a passion that his ethical reason condemns, we do not take this to be a defeat, rather a kind of terrible rebirth: at his latter end the artist knows a reality that he had until now refused to admit to consciousness.

Thoughts like these suggested that another of Nietzsche's works, *The Genealogy of Morals,* might be in point. It proposes a view of society which is consonant with the belief that art and not ethics constitutes the essential metaphysical activity of man and with the validation and ratification of the primitive energies. Nietzsche's theory of the social order dismisses all ethical impulse from its origins—the basis of society is to be found in the rationalization of cruelty: as simple as that. Nietzsche has no ultimate Utopian intention in saying this, no hope of revising the essence of the social order, although he does believe that its pain can be mitigated. He represents cruelty as a social necessity, for only by its exercise could men ever have been induced to develop a continuity of will: nothing else than cruel pain could have created in mankind that memory of intention which makes society possible. The method of cynicism which Nietzsche pursued—let us be clear that it is a method and not an attitude—goes so far as to describe punishment in terms of the pleasure derived from the exercise of cruety: "Compensation," he says, "consists in a legal warrant entitling one man to exercise his cruelty on another." There follows that most remarkable passage in which Nietzsche describes the process whereby the individual turns the cruety of punishment against himself and creates the bad conscience and the consciousness of guilt which manifests itself as a pervasive anxiety. Nietzsche's complexity of mind is beyond all comparison, for in this book which is dedicated to the liberation of the conscience, Nietzsche makes his defense of the bad conscience as a decisive force in the interests of culture. It is much the same line of argument that he takes when, having attacked the Jewish morality and the priestly existence in the name of the health of the spirit, he reminds us that only by his sickness does man become interesting.

From *The Genealogy of Morals* to Freud's *Civilization and Its Discontents* is but a step, and some might think that, for pedagogic purposes, the step is so small as to make the second book supererogatory. But although Freud's view of society and culture has indeed a very close affinity to Nietzsche's, Freud does add certain considerations which are essential to our sense of the modern disposition.

For one thing, he puts to us the question of whether or not we want to *accept* civilization. It is not the first time that the paradox of civilization has been present to the mind of civilized people, the sense that civilization makes men behave worse and suffer more than does some less developed state of human existence. But hitherto all such ideas were formulated in a moralizing way—civilization was represented as being "corrupt," a divagation from a state of innocence. Freud had no illusions about a primitive innocence, he conceived no practicable alternative to civilization. In consequence, there was a unique force to the question he asked: whether we wished to accept civilization, with all its contradictions, with all its pains—pains, for "discontents" does not accurately describe what Freud has in mind. He had his own answer to the question—his tragic, or stoic, sense of life dictated it: we do well to accept it, although we also do well to cast a cold eye on the fate that makes it our better part to accept it. Like Nietzsche, Freud thought that life was justified by our heroic response to its challenge.

But the question Freud posed has not been set aside or closed up by the answer that he himself gave to it. His answer, like Nietzsche's, is essentially in the line of traditional humanism—we can see this in the sternness with which he charges women not to interfere with men in the discharge of their cultural duty, not to claim men for love and the family to the detriment of their free activity in the world. But just here lies the matter of Freud's question that the world more and more believes Freud himself did not answer. The pain that civilization inflicts is that of the instinctual renunciation that civilization demands, and it would seem that fewer and fewer people wish to say with Freud that the loss of instinctual gratification, emotional freedom, or love, is compensated for either by the security of civilized life or by the stern pleasures of the masculine moral character.

With Freud's essay I brought to a close my list of prolegomenal books for the first term of the course. I shall not do much more than mention the books with which I introduced the second term, but I should like to do at least that. I began with *Rameau's Nephew*, thinking that the peculiar moral authority which Diderot assigns to the envious, untalented, unregenerate protagonist was peculiarly relevant to the line taken by the ethical explorations of modern literature. Nothing is more characteristic of the literature of our time than the replacement of the hero by what has come to be called the anti-hero, in whose indifference to or hatred of ethical nobility there is presumed to lie a special authenticity. Diderot is quite overt about this—he himself in his public character is the deuteragonist, the "honest consciousness," as Hegel calls him, and he takes delight in the discomfiture of the decent, dull person he is by the Nephew's nihilistic mind.

It seemed to me too that there was particular usefulness in the circumstance that this anti-hero should avow so openly his *envy,* which Tocqueville has called the ruling emotion of democracy, and that, although he envied anyone at all who had access to the creature-comforts and the social status which he lacked, what chiefly animated him was envy of men of genius. Ours is the first cultural epoch in which many men aspire to high achievement in the arts and, in their frustration, form a dispossessed class which cuts across the conventional class lines, making a proletariat of the spirit.

Although *Rameau's Nephew* was not published until fairly late in the century, it was known in manuscript by Goethe and Hegel; it suited the temper and won the admiration of Marx and Freud for reasons that are obvious. And there is ground for supposing that it was known to Dostoevski, whose *Notes from Underground* is a restatement of the essential idea of Diderot's dialogue in terms both more extreme and less genial. The Nephew is still on the defensive—he is naughtily telling secrets about the nature of man and society. But Dostoevski's underground man shouts aloud his envy and hatred and carries the ark of his self-hatred and alienation into a remorseless battle with what he calls "the good and the beautiful," mounting an attack upon every belief not merely of bourgeois society but of the whole humanist tradition. The inclusion of *Notes from Underground* among my prolegomenal books constituted something of a pedagogic risk, for if I wished to emphasize the subversive tendency of modern literature, here was a work which made all subsequent subversion seem like affirmation, so radical and so brilliant was its negation of our traditional pieties and its affirmation of our new pieties.

I hesitated in compunction before following *Notes from Underground* with Tolstoi's *Death of Ivan Ilyitch,* which so ruthlessly and with such dreadful force destroys the citadel of the commonplace life in which we all believe we can take refuge from ourselves and our fate. But I did assign it and then two of Pirandello's plays which, in the atmosphere of the sordidness of the commonplace life, undermine all the certitudes of the commonplace, common-sense mind.

From time to time I have raised with myself the question of whether my choice of these prolegomenal works was not extravagant, quite excessively tendentious. I have never been able to believe that it is. And if these works do indeed serve to indicate in an accurate way the nature of modern literature, a teacher might find it worth asking how his students respond to the strong dose.

One response I have already described—the readiness of the students to engage in the process that we might call the socialization of the anti-social, or the acculturation of the anti-cultural, or the legitimization of the subversive. When the term-essays come in, it is plain to me that almost none of the students have been taken aback by what they have read: they have wholly contained the attack. The chief exceptions are the few who simply do not comprehend, although they may be awed by, the categories of our discourse. In their papers, like poor hunted creates in a Kafka story, they take refuge first in misunderstood large phrases, then in bad grammar, then in general incoherence. After my pedagogical exasperation has run its course, I find that I am sometimes moved to give them a queer respect, as if they had stood up and said what in fact they don't have the wit to stand up and say: "Why do you harry us? Leave us alone. We are not Modern Man. We are the Old People. Ours is the Old Faith. We serve the little Old Gods, the gods of the copybook maxims, the small, dark, somewhat powerful deities of lawyers, doctors, engineers, accountants. With them is neither sensibility nor *angst.* With them is no disgust—it is they, indeed, who make ready the way for 'the good and the beautiful' about which low-minded doubts have been raised in this course, that 'good and beautiful' which we do not possess and don't want to possess but which we know justifies our lives. Leave us alone and let us worship our gods in the way they approve, in peace and unawareness." Crass, but—to use that interesting modern word which we have learned from the curators of museums—authentic. The rest, the minds that give me the A papers and the B papers and even the C+ papers, move through the terrors and mysteries of modern literature like so many Parsifals, asking no questions at the behest of wonder and fear. Or like so many seminarists who have been sytematically instructed in the constitution of Hell and the ways to damnation. Or like so many *readers,* entertained by moral horror stories. I asked them to look into the Abyss, and, both dutifully and gladly, they have looked into the Abyss, and the Abyss has greeted them with the grave courtesy of all objects of serious study, saying: "Interesting, am I not? And *exciting,* if you consider how deep I am and what dread beasts lie at my bottom. Have it well in mind that a knowledge of me contributes materially to your being whole, or well-rounded, men."

In my distress over the outrage I have conspired to perpetrate upon a great literature, I wonder if perhaps I have not been reading these papers too literally. After all, a term-essay is not a diary of the soul, it is not an occasion for telling the truth. What my students might reveal of their true feelings to a younger teacher they will not reveal to me; they will give me what they conceive to be the proper response to the official version of terror I have given them. I bring to mind their faces, which are not necessarily the faces of the authors of these unperturbed papers, nor are they, not yet, the faces of fathers of families, or of theatergoers, or of buyers of modern paintings: not yet. I must think it possible that in ways and to a degree which they keep secret they have responded directly and personally to what they have read.

And if they have? And if they have, am I the more content?

What form would I want their response to take? It is a teacher's question that I am asking, not a critic's. We have decided in recent years to think of the critic and the teacher of literature as one and the same, and no doubt it is both possible and useful to do so. But there are some points at which the functions of the two do not coincide, or can be made to coincide only with great difficulty. Of criticism we have been told, by Arnold, that "it must be apt to study and praise elements that for fulness of spiritual perfection are wanted, even though they belong to a power which in the practical sphere may be maleficent." But teaching, or at least undergraduate teaching, is not given the same licensed mandate—cannot be given it because the teacher's audience, which stands before his very eyes, as the critic's audience does not, asks questions about "the practical sphere," as the critic's audience does not. For instance, on the very day that I write this, when I had said to my class all I could think of to say about *The Magic Mountain* and invited questions and comments, one student asked, "How would you generalize the idea of the educative value of illness, so that it would be applicable not only to a particular individual, Hans Castorp, but to young people at large?" It makes us smile, but it was asked in all seriousness, and it is serious in its substance, and it had to be answered seriously, in part by the reflection that this idea, like so many ideas encountered in the books of the course, had to be thought of as having reference only to the private life; that it touched the public life only in some indirect or tangential way; that it really ought to be encountered in solitude, even in secrecy, since to talk about it in public and in our academic setting was to seem to propose for it a public practicality and thus to distort its meaning. To this another student replied; he said that, despite the public ritual of the classroom, each student inevitably experienced the books in privacy and found their meaning in reference to his own life. True enough, but the teacher sees the several privacies coming together to make a group, and they propose—no doubt the more because they come together every Monday, Wednesday, and Friday at a particular hour—the idea of a community, that is to say, "the practical sphere."

This being so, the teacher cannot escape the awareness of certain circumstances which the critic, who writes for an ideal, uncircumstanced reader, has no need to take into account. The teacher considers, for example, the social situation of his students—they are not of patrician origin, they do not come from homes in which stubbornness, pride, and conscious habit prevail, nor are they born into a culture marked by these traits, a culture in which other interesting and valuable things compete with and resist ideas; they come, mostly, from "good homes" in which authority and valuation are weak or at least not very salient and bold, so that ideas have for them, at their present stage of development, a peculiar power and preciousness. And in this connection the teacher will have in mind the special prestige that our culture, in its upper reaches, gives to art, and to the ideas that art proposes—the agreement, ever growing in assertiveness, that art yields more truth than any other intellectual activity. In this culture what a shock it is to encounter Santayana's acerb skepticism about art, or Keats's remark, which the critics and scholars never take notice of, presumably because they suppose it to be an aberration, that poetry is "not so fine a thing as philosophy— For the same reason that an eagle is not so fine a thing as a truth." For many students no ideas that they will encounter in any college discipline will equal in force and sanction the ideas conveyed to them by modern literature.

The author of *The Magic Mountain* once said that all his work could be understood as an effort to free himself from the middle class, and this, of course, will serve to describe the chief intention of all modern literature. And the means of freedom which Mann prescribes (the characteristic irony notwithstanding) is the means of freedom which in effect all of modern literature prescribes. It is, in the words of Clavdia Chauchat, *"se perdre et même . . . se laisser dépérir,"* and thus to name the means is to make plain that the end is not merely freedom from the middle class but freedom from society itself. I venture to say that the idea of losing oneself up to the point of self-destruction, of surrendering oneself to experience without regard to self-interest or conventional morality, of escaping wholly from the societal bonds, is an "element" somewhere in the mind of every modern person who dares to think of what Arnold in his unaffected Victorian way called "the fulness of spiritual perfection." But the teacher who undertakes to present modern literature to his students may not allow that idea to remain in the *somewhere* of his mind; he must take it from the place where it exists habitual and unrealized and put it in the conscious forefront of his thought. And if he is committed to an admiration of modern literature, he must also be committed to this chief idea of modern literature. I press the logic of the situation not in order to question the legitimacy of the commitment, or even the propriety of expressing the commitment in the college classroom (although it does seem odd!), but to confront those of us who do teach modern literature with the striking actuality of our enterprise.

Emma and the Legend
of Jane Austen

I T IS possible to say of Jane Austen, as perhaps we can say of no other writer, that the opinions which are held of her work are almost as interesting, and almost as important to think about, as the work itself. This statement, even with the qualifying "almost," ought to be, on its face, an illegitimate one. We all know that the reader should come to the writer with no preconceptions, taking no account of any previous opinion. But this, of course, he cannot do. Every established writer exists in the aura of his legend—the accumulated opinion that we cannot help being aware of, the image of his personality that has been derived, correctly or incorrectly, from what he has written. In the case of Jane Austen, the legend is of an unusually compelling kind. Her very name is a charged one. The homely quaintness of the Christian name, the cool elegance of the surname, seem inevitably to force upon us the awareness of her sex, her celibacy, and her social class. "Charlotte Brontë" rumbles like thunder and drowns out any such special considerations. But "Jane Austen" can by now scarcely fail to imply femininity, and, at that, femininity of a particular kind and in a particular social setting. It dismays many new readers that certain of her admirers call her Jane, others Miss Austen. Either appellation suggests an unusual, and questionable, relation with this writer, a relation that does not consort with the literary emotions we respect. The new reader perceives from the first that he is not to be permitted to proceed in simple literary innocence. Jane Austen is to be for him not only a writer but an issue. There are those who love her; there are those— no doubt they are fewer but they are no less passionate—who detest her; and the new reader understands that he is being solicited to a fierce partisanship, that he is required to make no mere literary judgment but a decision about his own character and personality, and about his relation to society and all of life.

And indeed the nature of the partisanship is most intensely personal and social. The matter at issue is: What kind of people like Jane Austen? What kind of people dislike her? Sooner or later the characterization is made or implied by one side or the other, and with extreme invidiousness. It was inevitable that there should arise a third body of opinion, which holds that it is not Jane Austen herself who is to be held responsible for the faults that are attributed to her by her detractors, but rather the people who admire her for the wrong reasons and in the wrong language and thus create a false image of her. As far back as 1905 Henry James was repelled by what a more recent critic, Professor Marvin Mudrick, calls "gentle-Janeism" and he spoke of it with great acerbity. James admired Jane Austen; his artistic affinity with her is clear, and he may be thought to have shared her social preferences and preoccupations. Yet James could say of her reputation that it had risen higher than her intrinsic interest warranted: the responsibility for this, he said, lay with "the body of publishers, editors, illustrators, producers of magazines, which have found their 'dear,' our dear, everybody's dear Jane so infinitely to their material purpose."[1] In our own day, Dr. Leavis's admiration for Jane Austen is matched in intensity by his impatience with her admirers. Mr. D. W. Harding in a well-known essay[2] has told us how the accepted form of admiration of Jane

[1] *The Question of Our Speech; The Lesson of Balzac: Two Lectures,* 1905.
[2] "Regulated Hatred: An Aspect of the Work of Jane Austen," *Scrutiny* VIII, March 1940.

Austen kept him for a long time from reading her novels, and how
he was able to be at ease with them only when he discovered that
they were charged with scorn of the very people who set the common tone of admiration. And Professor Mudrick, in the preface to
his book on Jane Austen,[3] speaks of the bulk of the criticism of her
work as being "a mere mass of cozy family adulation, self-
glorif[ication] . . . and nostalgic latterday enshrinements of the
gentle-hearted chronicler of Regency order." It is the intention of
Professor Mudrick's book to rescue Jane Austen from coziness and
nostalgia by representing her as a writer who may be admired for
her literary achievement, but who is not to be loved, and of whom it
is to be said that certain deficiencies of temperament account for
certain deficiencies of her literary practice.

The impatience with the common admiring view of Jane Austen
is not hard to understand and sympathize with, the less so because
(as Mr. Harding and Professor Mudrick say) admiration seems to
stimulate self-congratulation in those who give it, and to carry a
reproof of the deficient sensitivity, reasonableness, and even courtesy,
of those who withhold their praise. One may refuse to like almost
any author and incur no other blame from his admirers than that of
being wanting in taste in that one respect. But not to like Jane
Austen is to put oneself under suspicion of a general personal inadequacy and even—let us face it—of a want of breeding.

This is absurd and distasteful. And yet we cannot deal with this
unusual—this extravagantly personal—response to a writer simply in
the way of condemnation. No doubt every myth of a literary person
obscures something of the truth. But it may also express some part
of the truth as well. If Jane Austen is carried outside the proper
confines of literature, if she has been loved in a fashion that some
temperaments must find objectionable and that a strict. criticism
must call illicit, the reason is perhaps to be found not only in the
human weakness of her admirers, in their impulse to self-flattery, or
in whatever other fault produces their deplorable tone. Perhaps a

[3] *Jane Austen: Irony as Defense and Discovery*, 1952.

reason is also to be found in the work itself, in some unusual promise that it seems to make, in some hope that it holds out.

II

Of Jane Austen's six great novels *Emma* is surely the one that is
most fully representative of its author. *Pride and Prejudice* is of
course more popular. It is the one novel in the canon that "everybody" reads, the one that is most often reprinted. *Pride and Prejudice* deserves its popularity, but it is not a mere snobbery, an
affected aversion from the general suffrage, that makes thoughtful
readers of Jane Austen judge *Emma* to be the greater book—not the
more delightful but the greater. It cannot boast the brilliant, unim-
peded energy of *Pride and Prejudice,* but that is because the energy
which it does indeed have is committed to dealing with a more
resistant matter. In this it is characteristic of all three novels of Jane
Austen's mature period, of which it is the second. *Persuasion,* the
third and last, has a charm that is traditionally, and accurately, called
"autumnal," and it is beyond question a beautiful book. But *Persuasion,* which was published posthumously and which may not
have been revised to meet the author's full intention, does not have
the richness and substantiality of *Emma.* As for *Mansfield Park,* the
first work of the mature period, it quite matches *Emma* in point of
substantiality, but it makes a special and disturbing case. Greatly admired in its own day—far more than *Emma*—*Mansfield Park* is
now disliked by many readers who like everything else that Jane
Austen wrote. They are repelled by its heroine and by all that she
seems to imply of the author's moral and religious preferences at this
moment of her life, for Fanny Price consciously devotes herself to
virtue and piety, which she achieves by a willing submissiveness that
goes against the modern grain. What is more, the author seems to
be speaking out against wit and spiritedness (while not abating her
ability to represent these qualities), and virtually in praise of dullness
and acquiescence, and thus to be condemning her own peculiar

talents. *Mansfield Park* is an extraordinary novel, and only Jane Austen could have achieved its profound and curious interest, but its moral tone is antipathetic to contemporary taste, and no essay I have ever written has met with so much resistance as the one in which I tried to say that it was not really a perverse and wicked book. But *Emma,* as richly complex as *Mansfield Park,* arouses no such antagonism, and the opinion that holds it to be the greatest of all Jane Austen's novels is, I believe, correct.

Professor Mudrick says that everyone has misunderstood *Emma,* and he may well be right, for *Emma* is a very difficult novel. We in our time are used to difficult books and like them. But *Emma* is more difficult than any of the hard books we admire. The difficulty of Proust arises from the sheer amount and complexity of his thought, the difficulty of Joyce from the brilliantly contrived devices of representation, the difficulty of Kafka from a combination of doctrine and mode of communication. With all, the difficulty is largely literal; it lessens in the degree that we attend closely to what the books say; after each sympathetic reading we are the less puzzled. But the difficulty of *Emma* is never overcome. We never know where to have it. If we finish it at night and think we know what it is up to, we wake the next morning to believe it is up to something quite else; it has become a different book. Reginald Farrer speaks at length of the difficulty of *Emma* and then goes on to compare its effect with that of *Pride and Prejudice.* "While twelve readings of *Pride and Prejudice* give you twelve periods of pleasure repeated, as many readings of *Emma* give you that pleasure, not repeated only, but squared and squared again with each perusal, till at every fresh reading you feel anew that you never understood anything like the widening sum of its delights."[4] This is so, and for the reason that none of the twelve readings permits us to flatter ourselves that we have fully understood what the novel is doing. The effect is extraordinary, perhaps unique. The book is like a person—

[4] "Jane Austen," *Quarterly Review* 228, July 1917.

not to be comprehended fully and finally by any other person. It is perhaps to the point that it is the only one of Jane Austen's novels that has for its title a person's name.

For most people who recognize the difficulty of the book, the trouble begins with Emma herself. Jane Austen was surely aware of what a complexity she was creating in Emma, and no doubt that is why she spoke of her as "a heroine whom no one will like except myself." Yet this puts it in a minimal way—the question of whether we will like or not like Emma does not encompass the actuality of the challenge her character offers. John Henry Newman stated the matter more accurately, and very charmingly, in a letter of 1837. He says that Emma is the most interesting of Jane Austen's heroines, and that he likes her. But what is striking in his remark is this sentence: "I feel kind to her whenever I think of her." This does indeed suggest the real question about Emma, whether or not we will find it in our hearts to be kind to her.

Inevitably we are attracted to her, we are drawn by her energy and style, and by the intelligence they generate. Here are some samples of her characteristic tone:

"Never mind, Harriet, I shall not be a poor old maid; it is poverty only which makes celibacy contemptible to a generous public!"

Emma was sorry; to have to pay civilities to a person she did not like through three long months!—to be always doing more than she wished and less than she ought!

"I do not know whether it ought to be so, but certainly silly things do cease to be silly if they are done by sensible people in an impudent way. Wickedness is always wickedness, but folly is not always folly."

"Oh! I always deserve the best treatment, because I never put up with any other. . . ."

[On an occasion when Mr. Knightley comes to a dinner party in his carriage, as Emma thinks he should, and not on foot:] ". . . There is always a look of consciousness or bustle when people come in a way which they know to be beneath them. You think you carry it off very well, I dare say, but with you it is a sort of bravado, an air of affected unconcern; I always observe it whenever I meet you under these circumstances. *Now* you have nothing to try for. You are not afraid of being supposed ashamed. You are not striving to look taller than any body else. *Now* I shall really be happy to walk into the same room with you."

We cannot be slow to see what is the basis of this energy and style and intelligence. It is self-love. There is a great power of charm in self-love, although, to be sure, the charm is an ambiguous one. We resent it and resist it, yet we are drawn by it, if only it goes with a little grace or creative power. Nothing is easier to pardon than the mistakes and excesses of self-love: if we are quick to condemn them, we take pleasure in forgiving them. And with good reason, for they are the extravagance of the first of virtues, the most basic and biological of the virtues, that of self-preservation.

But we distinguish between our response to the self-love of men and the self-love of women. No woman could have won the forgiveness that has been so willingly given (after due condemnation) to the self-regard of, say, Yeats and Shaw. We understand self-love to be part of the moral life of all men; in men of genius we expect it to appear in unusual intensity and we take it to be an essential element of their power. The extraordinary thing about Emma is that she has a moral life as a man has a moral life. And she doesn't have it as a special instance, as an example of a new kind of woman, which is the way George Eliot's Dorothea Brooke has her moral life, but quite as a matter of course, as a given quality of her nature.

And perhaps that is what Jane Austen meant when she said that no one would like her heroine—and what Newman meant when he said that he felt kind to Emma whenever he thought of her. She needs kindness if she is to be accepted in all her exceptional actuality. Women in fiction only rarely have the peculiar reality of the moral life that self-love bestows. Most commonly they exist in a moonlike way, shining by the reflected moral light of men. They are "convincing" or "real" and sometimes "delightful," but they seldom exist as men exist—as genuine moral destinies. We do not take note of this; we are so used to the reflected quality that we do not observe it. It is only on the rare occasions when a female character like Emma confronts us that the difference makes us aware of the usual practice. Nor can we say that novels are deficient in realism when they present women as they do: it is the presumption of our society that women's moral life is not as men's. No change in the modern theory of the sexes, no advance in status that women have made, has yet contradicted this. The self-love that we do countenance in women is of a limited and passive kind, and we are troubled if it is as assertive as the self-love of men is permitted, and expected, to be. Not men alone, but women as well, insist on this limitation, imposing the requirement the more effectually because they are not conscious of it.

But there is Emma, given over to self-love, wholly aware of it and quite cherishing it. Mr. Knightley rebukes her for heedless conduct and says, "I leave you to your own reflections." And Emma wonderfully replies: "Can you trust me with such flatterers? Does my vain spirit ever tell me I am wrong?" She is 'Emma, never loth to be first," loving pre-eminence and praise, loving power and frank to say so.

Inevitably we are drawn to Emma. But inevitably we hold her to be deeply at fault. Her self-love leads her to be a self-deceiver. She can be unkind. She is a dreadful snob.

Her snobbery is of the first importance in her character, and it is of a special sort. The worst instance of it is very carefully chosen to put her thoroughly in the wrong. We are on her side when she mocks Mrs. Elton's vulgarity, even though we feel that so young a woman (Emma is twenty) ought not set so much store by manners and tone—Mrs. Elton, with her everlasting barouche-landau and her *"caro sposo"* and her talk of her spiritual "resources," is herself a snob in the old sense of the word, which meant a vulgar person aspiring to an inappropriate social standing. But when Emma presumes to look down on the young farmer, Robert Martin, and undertakes to keep little Harriet Smith from marrying him, she makes a truly serious mistake, a mistake of nothing less than national import.

Here it is to be observed that *Emma* is a novel that is touched—lightly but indubitably—by national feeling. Perhaps this is the result of the Prince Regent's having expressed his admiration for *Mansfield Park* and his willingness to have the author dedicate her next book to him: it is a circumstance which allows us to suppose that Jane Austen thought of herself, at this point in her career, as having, by reason of the success of her art, a relation to the national ethic. At any rate, there appears in *Emma* a tendency to conceive of a specifically English ideal of life. Knightley speaks of Frank Churchill as falling short of the demands of this ideal: "No, Emma, your amiable young man can be amiable only in French, not in English. He may be very 'aimable,' have very good manners, and be very agreeable; but he can have no English delicacy towards the feelings of other people: nothing really amiable about him." Again, in a curiously impressive moment in the book, we are given a detailed description of the countryside as seen by the party at Donwell Abbey, and this comment follows: "It was a sweet view—sweet to the eye and the mind. English verdure, English culture [agriculture, of course, is meant], English comfort, seen under a sun bright without being oppressive." This is a larger consideration than the occasion would appear to require; there seems no reason to expect this vision of "England's green and pleasant land." Or none until we note that the description of the view closes thus: ". . . and at the bottom of this bank, favourably placed and sheltered, rose the Abbey-Mill Farm, with meadows in front, and the river making a close and handsome curve around it." Abbey-Mill Farm is the property of young Robert Martin, for whom Emma has expressed a principled social contempt, and the little burst of strong feeling has the effect, among others, of pointing up the extremity of Emma's mistake.

It is often said, sometimes by way of reproach, that Jane Austen took no account in her novels of the great political events of her lifetime, nor of the great social changes that were going on in England. ". . . In Jane Austen's novels," says Arnold Hauser in his *Social History of Art,* "social reality was the soil in which characters were rooted but in no sense a problem which the novelist made any attempt to solve or interpret." The statement, true in some degree, goes too far. There is in *some* sense an interpretation of social problems in Jane Austen's contrivance of the situation of Emma and Robert Martin. The yeoman class had always held a strong position in English class feeling, and, at this time especially, only stupid or ignorant people felt privileged to look down upon it. Mr. Knightley, whose social position is one of the certainties of the book, as is his freedom from any trace of snobbery, speaks of young Martin, who is his friend, as a "gentleman farmer," and it is clear that he is on his way to being a gentleman pure and simple. And nothing was of greater importance to the English system at the time of the French Revolution that the relatively easy recruitment to the class of gentlemen. It made England unique among European nations. Here is Tocqueville's view of the matter as set forth in the course of his explanation of why England was not susceptible to revolution as France was:

It was not merely parliamentary government, freedom of speech, and the jury system that made England so different from the rest of contemporary Europe. There was something still more distinctive and more far-reaching in its effects. England was the only country in which the caste system had been totally abolished, not merely modified. Nobility and commoners joined forces in business enterprises, entered the same professions, and—what is still more significant—intermarried. The daughter of the greatest lord in the land could marry a "new" man without the least compunction. . . .

Though this curious revolution (for such in fact it was) is hidden in the mists of time, we can detect traces of it in the English language. For several centuries the word "gentleman" has had in England a quite different application from what it had when it originated. . . . A study of the connection between the history of language and history proper would certainly be revealing. Thus if we follow the mutation in time and place of the English word "gentleman" (a derivative of our *gentilhomme*), we find its connotation being steadily widened in England as the classes draw nearer to each other and intermingle. In each successive century we find it being applied to men a little lower in the social scale. Next, with the English, it crosses to America. And now in America, it is applicable to all male citizens, indiscriminately. Thus its history is the history of democracy itself.[5]

Emma's snobbery, then, is nothing less than a contravention of the best—and safest—tendency of English social life. And to make matters worse, it is a principled snobbery. "A young farmer . . . is the very last sort of person to raise my curiosity. The yeomanry are precisely the order of people with whom I feel that I can have nothing to do. A degree or two lower, and a creditable appearance might interest me; I might hope to be useful to their families in some way or other. But a farmer can need none of my help, and is therefore in one sense as much above my notice as in every other he is below it." This is carefully contrived by the author to seem as dreadful as possible; it quite staggers us, and some readers will even feel that the author goes too far in permitting Emma to make this speech.

Snobbery is the grossest fault that arises from Emma's self-love, but it is not the only fault. We must also take account of her capacity for unkindness. This can be impulsive and brutal, as in the witticism directed to Miss Bates at the picnic, which makes one of the most memorable scenes in the whole range of English fiction; or extended and systematic, as in her conspiracy with Frank Churchill to quiz Jane Fairfax. Then we know her to be a gossip, at least when she is tempted by Frank Churchill. She finds pleasure in dominating and has no compunctions about taking over the rule of Harriet Smith's life. She has been accused, on the ground of her

---

[5] Alexis de Tocqueville, *The Old Regime and the French Revolution*, Anchor edition, pp. 82–83. Tocqueville should not be understood as saying that there was no class system in England but only that there was no caste system, caste differing from class in its far greater rigidity. In his sense of the great advantage that England enjoyed, as compared with France, in having no caste system, Tocqueville inclines to represent the class feelings of the English as being considerably more lenient than in fact they were. Still, the difference between caste and class and the social and political importance of the "gentleman" are as great as Tocqueville says.

own estimate of herself, of a want of tenderness, and she has even been said to be without sexual responsiveness.

Why, then, should anyone be kind to Emma? There are several reasons, of which one is that we come into an unusual intimacy with her. We see her in all the elaborateness of her mistakes, in all the details of her wrong conduct. The narrative technique of the novel brings us very close to her and makes us aware of each misstep she will make. The relation that develops between ourselves and her becomes a strange one—it is the relation that exists between our ideal self and our ordinary fallible self. We become Emma's helpless conscience, her unavailing guide. Her fault is the classic one of *hubris,* excessive pride, and it yields the classic result of blindness, of an inability to interpret experience to the end of perceiving reality, and we are aware of each false step, each wrong conclusion, that she will make. Our hand goes out to hold her back and set her straight, and we are distressed that it cannot reach her.

There is an intimacy anterior to this. We come close to Emma because, in a strange way, she permits us to—even invites us to—by being close to herself. When we have said that her fault is *hubris* or self-love, we must make an immediate modification, for her self-love, though it involves her in self-deception, does not lead her to the ultimate self-deception—she believes she is clever, she insists she is right, but she never says she is good. A consciousness is always at work in her, a sense of what she ought to be and do. It is not an infallible sense, anything but that, yet she does not need us, or the author, or Mr. Knightley, to tell her, for example, that she is jealous of Jane Fairfax and acts badly to her; indeed, "she never saw [Jane Fairfax] without feeling that she had injured her." She is never offended—she never takes the high self-defensive line—when once her bad conduct is made apparent to her. Her sense of her superiority leads her to the "insufferable vanity" of believing "herself in the secret of everybody's feelings" and to the "unpardonable arrogance" of "proposing to arrange everybody's destiny," yet it is an innocent vanity and an innocent arrogance which, when frustrated and exposed, do not make her bitter but only ashamed. That is why, bad as

her behavior may be, we are willing to be implicated in it. It has
been thought that in the portrait of Emma there is "an air of
confession," that Jane Austen was taking account of "something
offensive" that she and others had observed in her own earlier manner and conduct, and whether or not this is so, it suggests the
quality of intimacy which the author contrives that we shall feel
with the heroine.

Then, when we try to explain our feeling of kindness to Emma,
we ought to remember that many of her wrong judgments and
actions are directed to a very engaging end, a very right purpose.
She believes in her own distinction and vividness and she wants all
around her to be distinguished and vivid. It is indeed unpardonable
arrogance, as she comes to see, that she should undertake to arrange
Harriet Smith's destiny, that she plans to "form" Harriet, making
her, as it were, the mere material or stuff of a creative act. Yet the
destiny is not meanly conceived, the act is meant to be truly creative—she wants Harriet to be a distinguished and not a commonplace person, she wants nothing to be commonplace, she requires of
life that it be well shaped and impressive, and alive. It is out of her
insistence that the members of the picnic shall cease being dull and
begin to be witty that there comes her famous insult to Miss Bates.
Her requirement that life be vivid is too often expressed in terms of
social deportment—she sometimes talks like a governess or a
dowager—but it is, in its essence, a poet's demand.

She herself says that she lacks tenderness, although she makes the
self-accusation in her odd belief that Harriet possesses this quality;
Harriet is soft and "feminine," but she is not tender. Professor
Mudrick associates the deficiency with Emma's being not susceptible to men. This is perhaps so; but if it is, there may be found in her
apparent sexual coolness something that is impressive and right. She
makes great play about the feelings and about the fineness of the
feelings that one ought to have; she sets great store by literature
(although she does not read the books she prescribes for herself)
and makes it a condemnation of Robert Martin that he does not

read novels. Yet although, like Don Quixote and Emma Bovary, her mind is shaped and deceived by fiction, she is remarkable for the actuality and truth of her sexual feelings. Inevitably she expects that Frank Churchill will fall in love with her and she with him, but others are more deceived in the outcome of this expectation than she is—it takes but little time for her to see that she does not really respond to Churchill, that her feeling for him is no more than the lively notice that an attractive and vivacious girl takes of an attractive and vivacious young man. Sentimental sexuality is not part of her nature, however much she feels it ought to be part of Harriet Smith's nature. When the right time comes, she chooses her husband wisely and seriously and eagerly.

There is, then, sufficient reason to be kind to Emma, and perhaps for nothing so much as the hope she expresses when she begins to understand her mistakes, that she will become "more acquainted with herself." And, indeed, all through the novel she has sought better acquaintance with herself, not wisely, not adequately, but assiduously. How modern a quest it is, and how thoroughy it confirms Dr. Leavis's judgment that Jane Austen is the first truly modern novelist of England. "In art," a critic has said, "the decision to be revolutionary usually counts for very little. The most radical changes have come from personalities who were conservative and even conventional . . ."[6] Jane Austen, conservative and even conventional as she was, perceived the nature of the deep psychological change which accompanied the establishment of democratic society—she was aware of the increase of the psychological burden of the individual, she understood the new necessity of conscious self-definition and self-criticism, the need to make private judgments of reality.[7] And there is no reality about which the modern person is more uncertain and more anxious than the reality of himself.

[6] Harold Rosenberg, "Revolution and the Idea of Beauty," *Encounter*, December 1953.
[7] See Abram Kardiner, *The Psychological Frontiers of Society*, 1945, page 410. In commenting on the relatively simple society which is described in James West's *Plainville, U.S.A.*, Dr. Kardiner touches on a matter which is dear, and

III

But the character of Emma is not the only reason for the difficulty of the novel. We must also take into account the particular genre to which the novel in some degree belongs—the pastoral idyll. It is an archaic genre which has the effect of emphasizing by contrast the brilliant modernity of Emma, and its nature may be understood through the characters of Mr. Woodhouse and Miss Bates.

These two people proved a stumbling-block to one of Jane Austen's most distinguished and devoted admirers, Sir Walter Scott. In his review of *Emma* in *The Quarterly Review,* Scott said that "characters of folly and simplicity, such as old Woodhouse and Miss Bates" are "apt to become tiresome in fiction as in real society." But Scott is wrong. Mr. Woodhouse and Miss Bates are remarkably interesting, even though they have been created on a system of character portrayal that is no longer supposed to have validity—they exist by reason of a single trait which they display whenever they appear. Miss Bates is possessed of continuous speech and of a perfectly free association of ideas which is quite beyond her control; once launched into utterance, it is impossible for her to stop. Mr. Woodhouse, Emma's father, has no other purpose in life than to preserve his health and equanimity, and no other subject of conversation than the means of doing so. The commonest circumstances of life present themselves to him as dangerous—to walk or to drive is to incur unwarrantable risk, to eat an egg not coddled in the prescribed way is to invite misery; nothing must ever change in his familial situation; he is appalled by the propensity of young people to marry, and to marry *strangers* at that.

---

all too dear, to Emma's heart—speaking of social mobility in a democratic, but not classless, society, he says that the most important criterion of class is "manners," that "knowing how to behave" is the surest means of rising in the class hierarchy. Nothing is more indicative of Jane Austen's accurate awareness of the mobility of her society than her concern not so much with manners themselves as with her characters' concern with manners.

Of the two "characters of folly and simplicity," Mr. Woodhouse is the more remarkable because he so entirely, so extravagantly, embodies a principle—of perfect stasis, of entire inertia. Almost in the degree that Jane Austen was interested in the ideal of personal energy, she was amused and attracted by persons capable of extreme inertness. She does not judge them harshly, as we incline to do—we who scarcely recall how important a part in Christian feeling the dream of *rest* once had. Mr. Woodhouse is a more extreme representation of inertness than Lady Bertram of *Mansfield Park*. To say that he represents a denial of life would not be correct. Indeed, by his fear and his movelessness, he affirms life and announces his naked unadorned wish to avoid death and harm. To life, to mere life, he sacrifices almost everything.

But if Mr. Woodhouse has a more speculative interest than Miss Bates, there is not much to choose between their achieved actuality as fictional characters. They are, as I have said, created on a system of character portrayal that we regard as primitive, but the reality of existence which fictional characters may claim does not depend only upon what they do, but also upon what others do to or about them, upon the way they are regarded and responded to. And in the community of Highbury, Miss Bates and Mr. Woodhouse are sacred. They are fools, to be sure, as everyone knows. But they are fools of a special and transcendent kind. They are innocents—of such is the kingdom of heaven. They are children, who have learned nothing of the guile of the world. And their mode of existence is the key to the nature of the world of Highbury, which is the world of the pastoral idyll. London is but sixteen miles away—Frank Churchill can ride there and back for a haircut—but the proximity of the life of London serves but to emphasize the spiritual geography of Highbury. The weather plays a great part in *Emma;* in no other novel of Jane Austen's is the succession of the seasons, and cold and heat, of such consequence, as if to make the point which the pastoral idyll characteristically makes, that the only hardships that man ought to have to endure are meteorological. In the Forest of Arden we suffer only "the penalty of Adam,/ The seasons' difference," and Amiens' song echoes the Duke's words:

> Here shall he see
> No enemy
> But winter and rough weather.

Some explicit thought of the pastoral idyll is in Jane Austen's mind, and with all the ambivalence that marks the attitude of *As You Like It* toward the dream of man's life in nature and simplicity. Mrs. Elton wants to make the strawberry party at Donwell Abbey into a *fête champêtre*: "It is to be a morning scheme, you know, Knightley; quite a simple thing. I shall wear a large bonnet, and bring one of my little baskets hanging on my arm. Here,—probably this basket with pink ribbon. Nothing can be more simple, you see. And Jane will have such another. There is to be no form or parade—a sort of gipsy party.—We are to walk about your gardens, and gather the strawberries ourselves, and sit under trees;—and whatever else you may like to provide, it is to be all out of doors—a table spread in the shade, you know. Every thing as natural and simple as possible. Is not that your idea?" To which Knightley replies: "Not quite. My idea of the simple and natural will be to have the table spread in the dining-room. The nature and the simplicity of gentlemen and ladies, with their servants and furniture, I think is best observed by meals within doors. When you are tired of eating strawberries in the garden, there will be cold meat in the house."

That the pastoral idyll should be mocked as a sentimentality by its association with Mrs. Elton, whose vulgarity in large part consists in flaunting the cheapened version of high and delicate ideals, and that Knightley should answer her as he does—this is quite in accordance with our expectation of Jane Austen's judgment. Yet it is only a few pages later that the members of the party walk out to see the view and we get that curious passage about the sweetness of the view, "sweet to the eye and to the mind." And we cannot help feeling that

"English verdure, English culture, English comfort, seen under a sun bright without being oppressive" make an England seen—if but for the moment—as an idyll.

The idyll is not a genre which nowadays we are likely to understand. Or at least not in fiction, the art which we believe must always address itself to actuality. The imagination of felicity is difficult for us to exercise. We feel that it is a betrayal of our awareness of our world of pain, that it is politically inappropriate. And yet one considerable critic of literature thought otherwise. Schiller is not exactly of our time, yet he is remarkably close to us in many ways and he inhabited a world scarcely less painful than ours, and he thought that the genre of the idyll had an important bearing upon social and political ideas. As Schiller defines it, the idyll is the literary genre that "presents the idea and description of an innocent and happy humanity."[8] This implies remoteness from the "artificial refinements of fashionable society"; and to achieve this remoteness poets have commonly set their idylls in actually pastoral surroundings and in the infancy of humanity. But the limitation is merely accidental—these circumstances "do not form the object of the idyll, but are only to be regarded as the most natural means to attain this end. The end is essentially to portray man in a state of innocence, which means a state of harmony and peace with himself and the external world." And Schiller goes on to assert the political importance of the genre: "A state such as this is not merely met with before the dawn of civilization; it is also the state to which civilization aspires, as to its last end, if only it obeys a determined tendency in its progress. The idea of a similar state, and the belief in the possible reality of this state, is the only thing that can reconcile man with all the evils to which he is exposed in the path of civilization. . . ."

It is the poet's function—Schiller makes it virtually the poet's political duty—to represent the idea of innocence in a "sensuous"

[8] "On Simple and Sentimental Poetry" in *Essays Aesthetical and Philosophical*, 1875.

way, that is, to make it seem real. This he does by gathering up the elements of actual life that do partake of innocence, and that the predominant pain of life leads us to forget, and forming them into a coherent representation of the ideal.[9]

But the idyll as traditionally conceived has an aesthetic deficiency of which Schiller is quite aware. Works in this genre, he says, appeal to the heart but not to the mind. ". . . We can only seek them and love them in moments in which we need calm, and not when our faculties aspire after movement and exercise. A morbid mind will find its *cure* in them, a sound soul will not find its *food* in them. They cannot vivify, they can only soften." For the idyll excludes the idea of activity, which alone can satisfy the mind—or at least the idyll as it has been traditionally conceived makes this exclusion, but Schiller goes on to imagine a transmutation of the genre in which the characteristic calm of the idyll shall be "the calm that follows accomplishment, not the calm of indolence—the calm that comes from the equilibrium reestablished between the faculties and not from the suspending of their exercise. . . ."

It is strange that Schiller, as he projects this new and as yet unrealized idea, does not recur to what he has previously said about comedy. To the soul of the writer of tragedy he assigns the adjective "sublime," which for him implies reaching greatness by intense effort and strength of will; to the soul of the writer of comedy he assigns the adjective "beautiful," which implies the achievement of freedom by an activity which is easy and natural. "The noble task of comedy," he says, "is to produce and keep up in us this freedom of mind." Comedy and the idyll, then, would seem to have a natural affinity with each other. Schiller does not observe this, but Shakespeare knew it—the curious power and charm of *As You Like It* consists of bringing the idyll and comedy together, of making the idyll the subject of comedy, even of satire, yet without negating it.

---

[9] Schiller, in speaking of the effectiveness that the idyll should have, does not refer to the pastoral-idyllic element of Christianity which represents Christ as an actual shepherd.

The mind teases the heart, but does not mock it. The unconditioned freedom that the idyll hypothecates is shown to be impossible, yet in the demonstration a measure of freedom is gained.

So in *Emma* Jane Austen contrives an idyllic world, or the closest approximation of an idyllic world that the genre of the novel will permit, and brings into contrast with it the actualities of the social world, of the modern self. In the precincts of Highbury there are no bad people, and no adverse judgments to be made. Only a modern critic, Professor Mudrick, would think to call Mr. Woodhouse an idiot and an old woman: in the novel he is called "the kind-hearted, polite old gentleman." Only Emma, with her modern consciousness, comes out with it that Miss Bates is a bore, and only Emma can give herself to the thought that Mr. Weston is *too* simple and openhearted, that he would be a "higher character" if he were not quite so friendly with everyone. It is from outside Highbury that the peculiarly modern traits of insincerity and vulgarity come, in the person of Frank Churchill and Mrs. Elton. With the exception of Emma herself, every person in Highbury lives in harmony and peace—even Mr. Elton would have been all right if Emma had let him alone!—and not merely because they are simple and undeveloped: Mr. Knightley and Mrs. Weston are no less innocent than Mr. Woodhouse and Miss Bates. If they please us and do not bore us by a perfection of manner and feeling which is at once lofty and homely, it is because we accept the assumptions of the idyllic world which they inhabit—we have been led to believe that man may actually live "in harmony and peace with himself and the external world."

The quiet of Highbury, the unperturbed spirits of Mr. Woodhouse and Miss Bates, the instructive perfection of Mr. Knightley and Mrs. Weston, constitute much of the charm of *Emma*. Yet the idyllic stillness of the scene and the loving celebration of what, for better or worse, is fully formed and changeless, is of course not what is decisive in the success of the novel. On the contrary, indeed: it is the idea of activity and development that is decisive. No one has put better and more eloquently what part this idea plays in Jane Austen's work than an anonymous critic writing in *The North British Review* in 1870:[10]

Even as a unit, man is only known to [Jane Austen] in the process of his formation by social influences. She broods over his history, not over his individual soul and its secret workings, nor over the analysis of its faculties and organs. She sees him, not as a solitary being completed in himself, but only as completed in society. Again, she contemplates virtues, not as fixed quantities, or as definable qualities, but as continual struggles and conquests, as progressive states of mind, advancing by repulsing their contraries, or losing ground by being overcome. Hence again the individual mind can only be represented by her as a battlefield where contending hosts are marshalled, and where victory inclines now to one side and now to another. A character therefore unfolded itself to her, not in statuesque repose, not as a model without motion, but as a dramatic sketch, a living history, a composite force, which could only exhibit what it was by exhibiting what it did. Her favourite poet Cowper taught her,

"By ceaseless action all that is subsists."

The mind as a battlefield: it does not consort with some of the views of Jane Austen that are commonly held. Yet this is indeed how she understood the mind. And her representation of battle is the truer because she could imagine the possibility of victory—she did not shrink from the idea of victory—and because she could represent harmony and peace.

The anonymous critic of *The North British Review* goes on to say a strange and startling thing—he says that the mind of Jane Austen was "saturated" with a "Platonic idea." In speaking of her ideal of "intelligent love"—the phrase is perfect—he says that it is based on the "Platonic idea that the giving and receiving of knowledge, the active formation of another's character, or the more passive growth under another's guidance, is the truest and strongest foundation of

[10] Volume LXXII, April, pp. 129-152. I am grateful to Professor Joseph Duffy for having told me of this admirable study.

love."[11] It is an ideal that not all of us will think possible of realization and that some of us will not want to give even a theoretical assent to. Yet most of us will consent to think of it as one of the most attractive of the idyllic elements of the novel. It proposes to us the hope of victory in the battle that the mind must wage, and it speaks of the expectation of allies in the fight, of the possibility of community—not in actuality, not now, but perhaps again in the future, for do we not believe, or almost believe, that there was community in the past?

The impulse to believe that the world of Jane Austen really did exist leads to notable error. "Jane Austen's England" is the thoughtless phrase which is often made to stand for the England of the years in which our author lived, although any serious history will make it sufficiently clear that the England of her novels was not the real England, except as it gave her the license to imagine the England which we call hers. This England, especially as it is represented in *Emma,* is an idyll. The error of identifying it with the actual England ought always to be remarked. Yet the same sense of actuality that corrects the error should not fail to recognize the remarkable force of the ideal that leads many to make the error. To represent the possibility of controlling the personal life, of becoming acquainted with ourselves, of creating a community of "intelligent love"—this is indeed to make an extraordinary promise and hold out a rare hope. We ought not be shocked and repelled if some among us think there really was a time when such promises and hopes were realized. Nor ought we be entirely surprised if, when they speak of the person who makes such promises and holds out such hopes, they represent her as not merely a novelist, if they find it natural to deal with her as a figure of legend and myth.

[11] Emma's attempt to form the character of Harriet is thus a perversion of the relation of Mrs. Weston and Mr. Knightley to herself—it is a perversion, says the *North British* critic, adducing Dante's *"amoroso uso de sapienza,"* because it is without love.

The Fate of Pleasure

OF ALL critical essays in the English language, there is none that has established itself so firmly in our minds as Wordsworth's Preface to *Lyrical Ballads*. Indeed, certain of the statements that the Preface makes about the nature of poetry have come to exist for us as something like proverbs of criticism. This is deplorable, for the famous utterances, in the form in which we hold them in memory, can only darken counsel. A large part of the literate world believes that Wordsworth defines poetry as the spontaneous overflow of powerful feelings. With such a definition we shall not get very far in our efforts to think about poetry, and in point of fact Wordsworth makes no such definition. Much less does he say, as many find it convenient to recall, that poetry is emotion recollected in tranquillity. Yet the tenacity with which we hold in mind our distortions of what Wordsworth actually does say suggests the peculiar power of the essay as a whole, its unique existence as a work of criticism. Its cogency in argument is notable, even if intermittent, but the Preface is not regarded by its readers only as an argument. By reason of its eloquence, and because of the impetuous spirit with which it engages the great questions of the nature and function of poetry, it presents itself to us not chiefly as a discourse, but rather as a dramatic action, and we are prepared to respond to its utterances less for their truth than for their happy boldness.

This being so, it should be a matter for surprise that one especially bold utterance of the Preface has not engaged us at all and is scarcely ever cited. I refer to the sentence in which Wordsworth speaks of what he calls "the grand elementary principle of pleasure," and says of it that it constitutes "the naked and native dignity of man," that it is the principle by which man "knows, and feels, and lives, and moves."

This is a statement which has great intrinsic interest, because, if we recognize that it is bold at all, we must also perceive that it is bold to the point of being shocking, for it echoes and controverts St. Paul's sentence which tells us that "we live, and move, and have our being" in God (Acts 17:28). And in addition to its intrinsic interest, it has great historical interest, not only because it sums up a characteristic tendency of eighteenth-century thought but also because it bears significantly upon a characteristic tendency of our contemporary culture. Its relation to that culture is chiefly a negative one—our present sense of life does not accommodate the idea of pleasure as something which constitutes the "naked and native dignity of man."

The word *pleasure* occurs frequently in the Preface. Like earlier writers on the subject, when Wordsworth undertakes to explain why we do, or should, value poetry, he bases his explanation upon the pleasure which poetry gives. Generally he uses the word in much the same sense that was intended by his predecessors. The pleasure which used commonly to be associated with poetry was morally unexceptionable and not very intense—it was generally understood that poetry might indeed sometimes excite the mind but only as a step toward composing it. But the word has, we know, two separate moral ambiences and two very different degrees of intensity. The pleasures of domestic life are virtuous; the pleasures of Imagination or Melancholy propose the idea of a cultivated delicacy of mind in those who experience them; the name of an English pipe-tobacco, "Parson's Pleasure," although derived from the place on the river at Oxford where men have traditionally bathed naked, is obviously meant to suggest that the word readily consorts with ideas of mildness. None of these point to what Byron had in mind when he wrote, "O pleasure! you're indeed a pleasant thing,/ Although one must be damn'd for you no doubt." The *Oxford English Dictionary* takes due note of what it calls an "unfavorable" sense of the word: "Sensuous enjoyment as a chief object of life, or end, in itself," and informs us that in this pejorative sense it is "sometimes personified as a female deity." The Oxford lexicographers do not stop there but go on to recognize what they call a "strictly physical" sense, which is even lower in the moral scale: "the indulgence of the appetites, sensual gratification." The "unfavorable" significations of the word are dramatized by the English career of the most usual Latin word for pleasure, *voluptas*. Although some Latin-English dictionaries, especially those of the nineteenth century, say that *voluptas* means "pleasure, enjoyment, or delight of body or mind in a good or a bad sense," the word as it was used in antiquity seems to have been on the whole morally neutral and not necessarily intense. But the English words derived from *voluptas* are charged with moral judgment and are rather excited. We understand that it is not really to the minds of men that a voluptuous woman holds out the promise of pleasure, enjoyment, or delight. We do not expect a voluptuary to seek his pleasures in domesticity, or in the Imagination of Melancholy, or in smoking a pipe.

It is obvious that any badness or unfavorableness of meaning that the word *pleasure* may have relates to the primitiveness of the enjoyment that is being referred to. Scarcely any moralist will object to pleasure as what we may call a secondary state of feeling, as a charm or grace added to the solid business of life. What does arouse strong adverse judgment is pleasure in its radical aspect, as it is the object of an essential and definitive energy of man's nature. It was because Bentham's moral theory represented pleasure in this way that Carlyle called it the Pig-philosophy. He meant, of course, that it impugned man's nature to associate it so immediately with pleasure. Yet this is just how Wordsworth asks us to conceive man's nature in the sentence I have spoken of—it is precisely pleasure in its primitive or radical aspect that he has in mind. He speaks of "the grand *elementary* principle of pleasure," which is to say, pleasure not as a mere charm or amenity but as the object of an instinct, of what Freud, whose complex exposition of the part that pleasure plays in life is of course much in point here, was later to call a *drive*. How little concerned was Wordsworth, at least in this one sentence, with pleasure in its mere secondary aspect is suggested by his speaking of it as constituting the *dignity* of man, not having in mind such dignity as is conferred by society but that which is *native* and *naked*.

When Carlyle denounced Bentham's assertion that pleasure is, and must be, a first consideration of the human being, it was exactly man's dignity that he was undertaking to defend. The traditional morality to which Carlyle subscribed was certainly under no illusion about the crude force of man's impulse to self-gratification, but it did not associate man's dignity with this force—on the contrary, dignity, so far as it was personal and moral, was thought to derive from the resistance which man offers to the impulse to pleasure.

For Wordsworth, however, pleasure was the defining attribute of life itself and of nature itself—pleasure is the "impulse from the vernal wood" which teaches us more of man and his moral being "than all the sages can." And the fallen condition of humanity— "what man has made of man"—is comprised by the circumstance that man alone of natural beings does not experience the pleasure which, Wordsworth believes, moves the living world. It is of course a commonplace of Wordsworth criticism that, although the poet set the highest store by the idea of pleasure, the actual pleasures he represents are of a quite limited kind. Certainly he ruled out pleasures that are "strictly physical," those which derive from "the indulgence of the appetites" and "sensual gratification," more particularly erotic gratification. His living world of springtime is far removed from that of Lucretius: nothing in it is driven by the irresistible power of *alma Venus*. This is not to say that there is no erotic aspect to Wordsworth's mind; but the eroticism is very highly sublimated—Wordsworth's pleasure always tended toward *joy,* a purer and more nearly transcendent state. And yet our awareness of this significant limitation does not permit us to underrate the boldness of

his statement in the Preface about the primacy of pleasure and the
dignity which derives from the principle of pleasure, nor to ignore
its intimate connection with certain radical aspects of the moral
theory of the French Revolution.[1]

For an understanding of the era of the Revolution, there is, I
think, much to be gained from one of the works of the German
economic historian Werner Sombart, whose chief preoccupation was
the origins of capitalism. In his extensive monograph, *Luxury and
Capitalism*, Sombart develops the thesis that the first great accumu-
lations of capital were achieved by the luxury trades in consequence
of that ever-increasing demand for the pleasures of the world, for
comfort, sumptuousness, and elegance, which is observed in Western Europe between the end of the Middle Ages and the end of the
eighteenth century. As a comprehensive explanation of the rise of
capitalism, this theory, I gather, has been largely discredited. Yet the
social and cultural data which Sombart accumulates are in themselves very interesting, and they are much to our point.

Sombart advances the view that the European preoccupation with
luxury took its rise in the princely courts and in the influence of
women which court life made possible; he represents luxury as
being essentially an expression of eroticism, as the effort to refine
and complicate the sexual life, to enhance, as it were, the quality of
erotic pleasure. The courtly luxury that Sombart studies is scarcely a
unique instance of the association of pleasure with power, of pleasure being thought of as one of the signs of power and therefore to
be made not merely manifest but conspicuous in the objects that
constitute the *décor* of the lives of powerful men—surely Egypt,
Knossos, and Byzantium surpassed Renaissance Europe in elaborateness of luxury. But what would seem to be remarkable about the
particular phenomenon that Sombart describes is the extent of its
proliferation at a certain period—the sheer amount of luxury that

1 And we ought not let go unheeded the explicit connection that Wordsworth
makes between poetry and sexuality. Explaining the pleasure of metrical language,
he says that it is "the pleasure which the mind derives from the perception of
similitude in dissimilitude." And he goes on: "This principle is the great spring
of the activity of our minds and their chief feeder. From this principle the direction
of the sexual appetite, and all the passions connected with it, take their origin."

got produced, its increasing availability to classes less than royal or noble, the overtness of the desire for it, and the fierceness of this desire. Sombart's data on these points are too numerous to be adduced here, but any tourist, having in mind what he has even casually seen of the secondary arts of Europe from the centuries in question, the ornaments, furniture, and garniture of certain stations of life, will know that Sombart does not exaggerate about the amount of luxury produced. And any reader of Balzac will recognize the intensity of the passions which at a somewhat later time attended the acquisition of elaborate and costly objects which were desired as the means or signs of pleasure.

What chiefly engages our interest is the influence that luxury may be discovered to have upon social and moral ideas. Such an influence is to be observed in the growing tendency of power to express itself mediately, by signs or indices, rather than directly, by the exercise of force. The richness and elaboration of the objects in a princely establishment were the indices of a power which was actual enough, but they indicated an actual power which had no need to avow itself in action. What a prince conceived of as his dignity might, more than ever before, be expressed by affluence, by the means of pleasure made overt and conspicuous.

And as the objects of luxury became more widely available, so did the dignity which luxury was meant to imply. The connection between dignity and a luxurious style of life was at first not self-evident—in France in 1670 the very phrase *bourgeois gentilhomme* was thought to be comical. In the contemporary English translation of the title of Molière's comedy, *The Cit Turned Gentleman*, it was funny too, but the English laugh was neither so loud nor so long as the French, with what good consequences for the English nation Tocqueville has made plain. Yet in France as in England, the downward spread of the idea of dignity, until it eventually became an idea that might be applied to man in general, was advanced by the increasing possibility of possessing the means or signs of pleasure. That idea, it need scarcely be said, established itself at the very heart of the radical thought of the eighteenth century. And Diderot himself, the most uncompromising of materialists, as he was the most subtle and delicate, could not have wanted a more categorical statement of his own moral and intellectual theory than Wordsworth's assertion that the grand elementary principle of pleasure constitutes the native and naked dignity of man, and that it is by this principle that man knows, and lives, and breathes, and moves.

Nothing so much connects Keats with Wordsworth as the extent of his conscious commitment to the principle of pleasure. But of course nothing so much separates Keats from his great master as his characteristic way of exemplifying the principle. In the degree that for Wordsworth pleasure is abstract and austere, for Keats it is explicit and voluptuous. No poet ever gave so much credence to the idea of pleasure in the sense of "indulgence of the appetites, sensual gratification," as Keats did, and the phenomenon that Sombart describes, the complex of pleasure-sensuality-luxury, makes the very fabric of his thought.

Keats's preoccupation with the creature-pleasures, as it manifests itself in his early work, is commonly regarded, even by some of his warmest admirers, with an amused disdain. At best, it seems to derive from the kind of elegant minuscule imagination that used to design the charming erotic scenes for the lids of enameled snuff boxes. At worst, in the explicitness of its concern with luxury, it exposes itself to the charge of downright vulgarity that some readers have made. The word *luxury* had a charm for Keats, and in his use of it he seems on the point of reviving its older meaning, which is specifically erotic and nothing but erotic; for Chaucer and Shakespeare *luxury* meant lust and its indulgence. Women present themselves to Keats's imagination as luxuries: "All that soft luxury/ that nestled in his arms." A poem is described as "a posy/ Of luxuries, bright, milky, soft and rosy." Poetry itself is defined by reference to objects of luxury, and even in its highest nobility, its function is said to be that of comforting and soothing.

Nor is the vulgarity—if we consent to call it that—confined to the early works; we find it in an extreme form in a poem of Keats's maturity. The lover in *Lamia* is generally taken to be an innocent youth, yet the most corrupt young man of Balzac's scenes of Parisian life would scarcely have spoken to his mistress or his fiancée as Lycius speaks to Lamia when he insists that she display her beauty in public for the enhancement of his prestige. Tocqueville said that envy was the characteristic emotion of plutocratic democracy, and it is envy of a particularly ugly kind that Lycius wishes to excite. "Let my foes choke," he says, "and my friends shout afar,/ While through the thronged streets your bridal car/ Wheels round its dazzling spokes." I am not sure that we should be at pains to insist that this is wholly a dramatic utterance and not a personal one, that we ought entirely to dissociate Keats from Lycius. I am inclined to think that we should suppose Keats to have been involved in all aspects of the principle of pleasure, even the ones that are vulgar and ugly. Otherwise we miss the full complication of that dialectic of pleasure which is the characteristic intellectual activity of Keats's poetry.

The movement of this dialectic is indicated in two lines from an early poem in which Keats speaks of "the pillowy silkiness that rests/ Full in the speculation of the stars"—it is the movement from the sensual to the transcendent, from pleasure to knowledge, and knowledge of an ultimate kind. Keats's intellect was brought into fullest play when the intensity of his affirmation of pleasure was met by the intensity of his skepticism about pleasure. The principle of pleasure is for Keats, as it is for Wordworth, the principle of reality—by it, as Wordsworth said, we *know*. But for Keats it is also the principle of illusion. In *The Eve of St. Agnes*, to take the most obvious example, the moment of pleasure at the center of the poem, erotic pleasure expressed in the fullest possible imagination of the luxurious, is the very essence of reality: it is all we know on earth and all we need to know. And it is the more real as reality and it is the more comprehensive as knowledge exactly because in the poem it exists surrounded by what on earth denies it, by darkness, cold, and death, which make it transitory, which make the felt and proclaimed reality mere illusion.

But we must be aware that in Keats's dialectic of pleasure it is not only external circumstances that condition pleasure and bring it into question as the principle of reality, but also the very nature of pleasure itself. If for Keats erotic enjoyment is the peak and crown of all pleasures, it is also his prime instance of the way in which the desire for pleasure denies itself and produces the very opposite of itself.

> Love in a hut, with water and a crust,
> Is—Love, forgive us—cinders, ashes, dust;
> Love in a palace is perhaps at last
> More grievous torment than a hermit's fast.

This opening statement of the second part of *Lamia* is not, as it is often said to be, merely a rather disagreeable jaunty cynicism but one of Keats's boldest expressions of his sense that there is something perverse and self-negating in the erotic life, that it is quite in the course of nature that we should feel "Pleasure . . . turning to Poison as the bee-mouth sips." He insists on the seriousness of the statement in a way that should not be hard to interpret—referring to the lines I have just quoted, he says

> That is a doubtful tale from faery land,
> Hard for the non-elect to understand.

That faery land we know very well—in the Nightingale Ode, Keats's epithet for the region is *forlorn;* it is the country of La Belle Dame sans Merci, the scene of erotic pleasure which leads to devastation, of an erotic fulfillment which implies castration.

Keats, then, may be thought of as the poet who made the boldest affirmation of the principle of pleasure and also as the poet who brought the principle of pleasure into the greatest and *sincerest* doubt. He therefore has for us a peculiar cultural interest, for it would seem to be true that at some point in modern history the principle of pleasure came to be regarded with just such ambivalence.

This divided state of feeling may be expressed in terms of a breach between politics and art. Modern societies seek to fulfill themselves in affluence, which of course implies the possibility of pleasure. Our political morality is more than acquiescent to this intention. Its simple and on the whole efficient criterion is the extent to which affluence is distributed among individuals and nations. But another morality, which we may describe as being associated with art, regards with a stern and even minatory gaze all that is implied by affluence, and it takes a dim or at best a very complicated view of the principle of pleasure. If we speak not only of the two different modes of morality, the political and the artistic, but also of the people who are responsive to them, we can say that it is quite within the bounds of possibility, if not of consistency, for the same person to respond, and intensely, to both of the two moral modes: it is by no means uncommon for an educated person to base his judgment of politics on a simple affirmation of the principle of pleasure, and to base his judgment of art, and also his judgment of personal existence, on a complex antagonism to that principle. This dichotomy makes one of the most significant circumstances of our cultural situation.

A way of testing what I have said about the modern artistic attitude to pleasure is afforded by the conception of poetry which Keats formulates in "Sleep and Poetry." This poem does not express everything that Keats thought about the nature and function of poetry, but what it does express is undeniably central to his thought, and for the modern sensibility it is inadmissible and even repulsive. It tells us that poetry is gentle, soothing, cheerful, healthful, serene, smooth, regal; that the poet, in the natural course of his development, will first devote his art to the representation of the pleasures of appetite, of things that can be bitten and tasted, such as apples, strawberries, and the white shoulders of nymphs, and that he will give his attention to the details of erotic enticement amid grateful sights and odors, and to sexual fulfillment and sleep. The poem then goes on to say that, as the poet grows older, he will write a different kind of poetry, which is called nobler; this later kind of poetry is less derived from and directed to the sensuality of youth and is more fitted to the gravity of mature years, but it still ministers to pleasure and must therefore be strict in its avoidance of ugly themes; it must not deal with those distressing matters which are referred to as "the burrs and thorns of life"; the great end of poetry, we are told, is "to soothe the cares, and lift the thoughts of man."

Such doctrine from a great poet puzzles and embarrasses us. It is, we say, the essence of Philistinism.

The conception of the nature and function of poetry which Keats propounds is, of course, by no means unique with him—it can be understood as a statement of the common assumptions about art which prevailed through the Renaissance up to some point in the nineteenth century, when they began to lose their force.[2] Especially in the eighteenth century, art is closely associated with luxury—with the pleasure or at least the comfort of the consumer, or with the quite direct flattery of his ego. The very idea of Beauty seems to imply considerations of this sort, which is perhaps why the eighteenth century was so much drawn to the idea of the Sublime, for that word would seem to indicate a kind of success in art which could not be called Beauty because it lacked the smoothness and serenity (to take two attributes from Keats's catalogue) and the immediacy of gratification which the idea of Beauty seems to propose. But the Sublime itself of course served the purposes of egoism—thus, that instance of the Sublime which was called the Grand Style, as it is described by its great English exponent in painting, Sir Joshua Reynolds, is said to be concerned with "some instance of heroic action or heroic suffering" and its proper effect, Reynolds explains, is to produce the emotion which Bouchardon reported he felt when he read Homer: "His whole frame appeared to himself to be enlarged, and all nature which surrounded him diminished to atoms."[3]

---

[2] One of the last significant exponents of the old assumptions was the young Yeats. He was "in all things pre-Raphaelite"—a partisan, that is, not of the early and austere pre-Raphaelite mode, but of the later sumptuous style, tinged with a sort of mystical eroticism—and he stubbornly resisted the realism of Carolus Duran and Bastien-Lepage, which was being brought back to England by the painters who had gone to study in Paris. His commitment to the "beautiful," as against truthful ugliness, was an issue of great moment between him and his father.

[3] All writers on the Sublime say in effect what Bouchardon says—that, although the sublime subject induces an overpowering emotion, even fear or terror, it does

In connection with the art of the eighteenth century I used the disagreeable modern word *consumer*, meaning thus to suggest the affinity that art was thought to have with luxury, its status as a commodity which is implied by the solicitude it felt for the pleasure and the comfort of the person who was to own and experience it. Certainly Wordsworth was pre-eminent in the movement to change this state of affairs,[4] yet Wordsworth locates the value of metrical language as lying in its ability to protect the reader from the discomfort of certain situations that poetry may wish to represent and he compares the effect of such situations in novels with their effect in Shakespeare, his point being that in novels they are "distressful" but in Shakespeare they are not.[5] It was, we know, an explanation which did not satisfy Keats, who was left to puzzle out why it is that in *King Lear* "all disagreeables evaporate." He discovers that this effect is achieved by "intensity," and we of our day are just at the point of being comfortable with him when he disappoints our best hopes by hedging: he is constrained to say that the "disagree-

---

so in a way that permits us to rise superior to it and thus gives us occasion to have a good opinion of our power of intellect and of ourselves generally. The Sublime has this direct relation to comfort and luxury, that it induces us "to regard as small those things of which we are wont to be solicitous" (Kant, *Critique of Aesthetic Judgment*). A more ambitious treatment of my subject would require a much fuller exposition of the theory of the Sublime. Of this theory, which so much occupied the writers on art of the eighteenth century, it can be said that it has much more bearing upon our own literature than modern critics have recognized. The classic study in English is Samuel H. Monk's *The Sublime*, first published in 1935, recently reissued as an Ann Arbor Paperback.

[4] ". . . Men . . . who talk of Poetry as a matter of amusement and idle pleasure; who will converse with us as gravely about a *taste* for Poetry, as they express it, as if it were a thing as indifferent as a taste for rope-dancing, or Frontiniac, or Sherry."

[5] The strength of Wordsworth's impulse to suppress the "distressful" is suggested by the famous passage in *The Prelude* in which the poet explains how his childhood reading served to inure him to the terrors of actuality. He recounts the incident, which occurred when he was nine years old, of his seeing a drowned man brought up from the bottom of Esthwaite Lake. He was, he says, not overcome by fear of the "ghastly face," because his "inner eye" had seen such sights before in fairy tales and romances. And then he feels it necessary to go further, to go beyond the bounds of our ready credence, for he tells us that from his reading came "a spirit" which hallowed the awful sight

> With decoration and ideal grace
> A dignity, a smoothness, like the works
> Of Grecian Art, and purest poetry.

ables" evaporate not only by the operation of intensity but also by "their being in close connection with Beauty & Truth." But we do at last find ourselves at one with him when, in his sonnet "On Sitting Down to Read King Lear Once Again," he dismisses all thought of pleasure and prepares himself for the pain he is in duty bound to undergo:

> . . . Once again, the fierce dispute
> Betwixt damnation and impassion'd clay
> Must I burn through; once more humbly assay
> The bitter-sweet of this Shakespearian fruit.

He is by no means certain that the disagreeables really will evaporate and that he will emerge whole and sound from the experience, and he prays to Shakespeare and "the clouds of Albion" that they will guard him against wandering "in a barren dream," and that, when he is "consumed in the fire," they will contrive his Phoenix-resurrection.

This we of our time can quite understand. We are repelled by the idea of an art that is consumer-directed and comfortable, let alone luxurious. Our typical experience of a work which will eventually have authority with us is to begin our relation to it at a conscious disadvantage, and to wrestle with it until it consents to bless us. We express our high esteem for such a work by supposing that it judges us. And when it no longer does seem to judge us, or when it no longer baffles and resists us, when we begin to feel that we *possess* it, we discover that its power is diminished. In our praise of it we are not likely to use the word *beauty:* we consented long ago—more than four decades ago—to the demonstration made by I. A. Richards in collaboration with Ogden and Wood that the concept of Beauty either could not be assigned any real meaning, or that it was frivolously derived from some assumed connection between works of art and our sexual preferences, quite conventional sexual preferences at that. "Beauty: it curves: curves are beauty," says Leopold Bloom, and we smile at so outmoded an aesthetic—how like him! With a similar amusement we read the language in which the young Yeats praised beauty in *The Secret Rose* (1896)—he speaks of those who are so fortunate as to be "heavy with the sleep/ Men have named beauty."[6]

In short, our contemporary aesthetic culture does not set great store by the principle of pleasure in its simple and primitive meaning and it may even be said to maintain an antagonism to the principle of pleasure. Such a statement of course has its aspect of absurdity, but in logic only. There is no psychic fact more available to our modern comprehension than that there are human impulses which, in one degree or another, and sometimes in the very highest degree, repudiate pleasure and seek gratification in—to use Freud's word—unpleasure.

The repudiation of pleasure in favor of the gratification which may be found in unpleasure is a leading theme of Dostoevski's great *nouvelle, Notes from Underground.* Of this extraordinary work Thomas Mann has said that "its painful and scornful conclusions," its "radical frankness . . . ruthlessly transcending all novelistic and literary bounds," have "long become parts of our moral culture." Mann's statement is accurate but minimal—the painful and scornful conclusions of Dostoevski's story have established themselves not only as parts of our moral culure but as its essence, at least so far as that culture makes itself explicit in literature.

Notes from Underground is an account, given in the first person, of the temperament and speculations of a miserable clerk, disadvantaged in every possible way, who responds to his unfortunate plight

---

[6] Mr. Bloom's observation (which goes on to "shapely goddesses Venus, Juno: curves the world admires" and "lovely forms of women sculped Junonian") follows upon his lyrical recollection of his first sexual encounter with Molly; Yeats's phrase occurs in the course of a poem to Maud Gonne. I think it is true to say of Joyce (at least up through *Ulysses*) and of Yeats that they were among the last devotees of the European cult of Woman, of a Female Principle which, in one way or another, *ziegt uns hinan,* and that Molly and Maud are perhaps the last women in literature to be represented as having a transcendent and on the whole beneficent significance (although Lara in *Dr. Zhivago* should be mentioned—it is she who gives that novel much of its archaic quality). The radical change in our sexual mythos must surely be considered in any speculation about the status of pleasure in our culture. It is to the point, for example, that in Kafka's account of the spiritual life, which is touched on below, women play a part that is at best ambiguous.

by every device of bitterness and resentment, by hostility toward those of mankind who are more unfortunate than he is, and also by the fiercest contempt for his more fortunate fellow beings, and for the elements of good fortune. He hates all men of purposeful life, and reasonable men, and action, and happiness, and what he refers to as "the sublime and the beautiful," and pleasure. His mind is subtle, complex, and contradictory almost beyond credibility—we never know where to have him and in our exhaustion we are likely to explain his perversity in some simple way, such as that he hates because he is envious, that he despises what he cannot have: all quite natural. But we are not permitted to lay this flattering unction to our souls—for one thing, he himself beats us to that explanation. And although it is quite true, it is only a small part of the truth. It is also true that he does not have because he does not wish to have; he has arranged his own misery—arranged it in the interests of his dignity, which is to say, of his freedom. For to want what is commonly thought to be appropriate to men, to want whatever it is, high or low, that is believed to yield pleasure, to be active about securing it, to use common sense and prudence to the end of gaining it, this is to admit and consent to the *conditioned* nature of man. What a distance we have come in the six decades since Wordworth wrote his Preface! To know and feel and live and move at the behest of the principle of pleasure—this, for the Underground Man, so far from constituting his native and naked dignity, constitutes his humiliation in bondage. It makes him, he believes, a mechanic thing, the puppet of whoever or whatever can offer him the means of pleasure. If pleasure is indeed the principle of his being, he is as *known* as the sum of 2 and 2; he is a mere object of reason, of that rationality of the revolution which is established upon the primacy of the principle of pleasure.

At one point in his narrative, the protagonist of *Notes from Underground* speaks of himself as an "anti-hero." He is the eponymous ancestor of a now-numerous tribe. He stands as the antagonistic opposite to all the qualities which are represented by that statue of

Sophocles which Professor Margarete Bieber tells us we are to have in mind when we try to understand the Greek conception of the hero, the grave beauty of the countenance and physique expressing the strength and order of the soul; the Underground Man traces his line of descent back to Thersites. It is in his character of anti-hero that he addresses the "gentlemen," as he calls them, the men of action and reason, the lovers of "the sublime and the beautiful," and brags to them, "I have more life in me than you have."

More life: perhaps it was this boast of the Underground Man that Nietzsche recalled when he said, Dostoevski's Underman and my Overman are the same person clawing his way out of the pit [of modern thought and feeling] into the sunlight." One understands what Nietzsche meant, but he is mistaken in the identification, for his own imagination is bounded on one side by that word *sunlight,* by the Mediterranean world which he loved: by the tradition of humanism with its recognition of the value of pleasure. He is ineluctably constrained by considerations of society and culture, however much he may despise his own society and culture, but the Underground Man is not. To be sure, the terms of the latter's experience are, in the first instance, social; he is preoccupied by questions of status and dignity, and he could not, we may suppose, have come into existence if the fates of the heroes of Balzac and Stendhal had not previously demonstrated that no object of desire or of the social will is anything but an illusion and a source of corruption, society being what it is. But it is the essence of the Underground Man's position that his antagonism to society arises not in response to the deficiencies of social life, but, rather, in response to the insult society offers his freedom by aspiring to be beneficent, to embody "the sublime and the beautiful" as elements of its being. The anger Dostoevski expresses in *Notes from Underground* was activated not by the bad social condition of Russia in 1864 but by the avowed hope of some people that a good social condition could be brought into being. A Utopian novel of the day, Chernyshevski's *What Is to Be Done?*, seemed to him an especially repugnant expression of this hope.[7] His disgust was aroused by this novel's assumption that man would be better for a rationally organized society, by which was meant, of course, a society organized in the service of pleasure. Dostoevski's reprobation of this idea, begun in *Notes from Underground,* reached its climax in Ivan Karamazov's poem of the Grand Inquisitor, in which again, but this time without the brilliant perversities of the earlier work, the disgust with the specious good of pleasure serves as the ground for the affirmation of spiritual freedom.

I have taken the phrase "specious good" from a passage in Wallace Fowlie's little book on Rimbaud, in which Mr. Fowlie discusses what he calls "the modern seizure and comprehension of spirituality." Without evasion, Mr. Fowlie identifies a chief characteristic of our culture which critics must inevitably be conscious of and yet don't like to name. If we are to be aware of the spiritual intention of modern literature, we have to get rid of certain nineteenth-century connotations of the word *spiritual*, all that they may imply to us of an overrefined and even effeminate quality, and have chiefly in mind what Mr. Fowlie refers to when he speaks of a certain type of saint and a certain type of poet and says of them that "both the saint and the poet exist through some propagation of destructive violence." And Mr. Fowlie continues: "In order to discover what is the center of themselves, the saint has to destroy the world of evil, and the poet has to destroy the world of specious good."

7 "A Utopian novel of the day" does not, of course, give anything like an adequate notion of the book's importance in the political culture of Russia. Dostoevski chose his antagonist with the precision that was characteristic of him, for Chernyshevski, who thought of himself as the heir of the French Enlightenment, by his one novel exercised a decisive influence upon the Russian revolutionaries of the next two generations, most notably upon Lenin, who borrowed its title for one of his best-known pamphlets and whose moral style was much influenced by the character Rakhmétov. This paragon of revolutionists, although very fond of the luxury in which he was reared, embraces an extreme asceticism because, as he says, "We demand that men may have a complete enjoyment of their lives, and we must show by our example that we demand it, not to satisfy our personal passions, but for mankind in general; that what we say we say from principle and not from passion, from conviction and not from personal desire." Only one pleasure is proof against Rakhmétov's iron will—he cannot overcome his love of expensive cigars.

The destruction of what is considered to be specious good is surely one of the chief literary enterprises of our age. Whenever in modern literature we find violence, whether of represented act or of expression, and an insistence upon the sordid and the disgusting, and an insult offered to the prevailing morality or habit of life, we may assume that we are in the presence of the intention to destroy specious good, that we are being confronted by that spirituality, or the aspiration toward it, which subsists upon violence against the specious good.

The most immediate specious good that a modern writer will seek to destroy is, of course, the habits, manners, and "values" of the bourgeois world, and not merely because these associate themselves with much that is bad, such as vulgarity, or the exploitation of the disadvantaged, but for other reasons as well, because they clog and hamper the movement of the individual spirit toward freedom, because they prevent the attainment of "more life." The particular systems and modes of thought of the bourgeois world are a natural first target for the modern spirituality. But it is not hard to believe that the impulse to destroy specious good would be as readily directed against the most benign socialist society, which, by modern definition, serves the principle of pleasure.

In the characteristically modern conception of the spiritual life, the influence of Dostoevski is definitive. By comparison with it, the influence of Nietzsche is marginal. The moral and personal qualities suggested by a particular class, the aristocracy, had great simple force with Nietzsche and proposed to his imagination a particular style of life. Despite the scorn he expressed for liberal democracy and socialist theory as he knew them, he was able to speak with sympathy of future democracies and possible socialisms, led to do so by that element of his thought which served to aerate his mind and keep it frank and generous—his awareness of the part played in human existence by the will to power, which, however it figures in the thought of his epigones and vulgarizers, was conceived by Nietzsche himself as comprising the whole range of the possibilities of human energy, creativity, libido. The claims of any social group to this human characteristic had weight with him. And he gave ready credence to the pleasure that attends one or another kind of power; if he was quick to judge people by the pleasures they chose— and woe to those who preferred beer to wine and *Parsifal* to *Carmen!*—the principle of pleasure presented itself to him as constituting an element of the dignity of man. It is because of this humanism of his, this naturalistic acceptance of power and pleasure, that Nietzsche is held at a distance by the modern spiritual sensibility. And the converse of what explains Nietzsche's relative marginality explains Dostoevski's position at the very heart of the modern spiritual life.

If we speak of spirituality, we must note that it is not only humanism that is negated by the Underground Man but Christianity as well, or at least Christianity as Western Europe understands it. For not only humanism but the Christianity of the West bases reason upon pleasure, upon pleasure postponed and purified but analogous in kind to worldly pleasure. Dostoevski's clerk has had his way with us: it would seem to be true that, in the degree that the promises of the spiritual life are made in terms of pleasure—of comfort, rest, and beauty—they have no power over the modern imagination. If Kafka, perhaps more than any other writer of our time, lends the color of reality to the events of the spiritual life, his power to do so lies in his characterizing these events by unpleasure, by sordidness and disorder, even when, as in *The Castle,* the spiritual struggle seems to yield a measure of success. He understood that a divinity who, like Saint Augustine's, could be spoken of as gratifying all the senses, must nowadays be deficient in reality and that a heaven which is presented to us as well ordered, commodious, beautiful—as *luxurious*—cannot be an object of hope. Yeats tells us that "Berkeley in his youth described the summum bonum and the reality of Heaven as physical pleasure, and thought this conception made both more intelligible to simple men." To simple men perhaps, but who now is a simple man? How far from our imagination is the idea of "peace" as the crown of spiritual struggle! The idea of "bliss" is even further removed. The two words propose to us a state of virtually infantile passivity which is the negation of the "more life" that we crave, the "more life" of spiritual militancy. We dread Eden, and of all Christian concepts there is none we understand so well as the *felix culpa* and the "fortunate fall"; not, certainly, because we anticipate the salvation to which these Christian paradoxes point, but because by means of the sin and the fall we managed to escape the seductions of peace and bliss.

My first intention in trying to make explicit a change in the assumptions of literature which everybody is more or less aware of has been historical and objective. But it must be obvious that my account of the change has not been wholly objective in the sense of being wholly neutral. It asks a question which is inevitably adversary in some degree, if only by reason of the irony which is implicit in the historical approach to a fact of moral culture. It suggests that the modern spirituality, with its devaluation of the principle of pleasure, because it came into being at a particular time, may be regarded as a contingent and not a necessary mode of thought. This opens the way to regarding it as a mode of thought which is "received" or "established" and which is therefore, like any other received or established mode of thought, available to critical scrutiny.

And that possibility is by no means comfortable. We set great store by the unillusioned militancy of spirit which deals violently with the specious good. Upon it we base whatever self-esteem we can lay claim to—it gives us, as one of D. H. Lawrence's characters says of it (or something very much like it), our "last distinction"; he feels that to question it is a "sort of vulgarity."[8] To what end, with what intention, is it to be questioned? Can an adversary scrutiny of it point away from it to anything else than an idiot literature, to "positive heroes" who know how to get the good out of life and who have "affirmative" emotions about their success in doing so? The energy, the consciousness, and the wit of modern literature

[8] Gerald Crich, in Chapter XXIX of *Women in Love*.

derive from its violence against the specious good. We instinctively resent questions which suggest that there is fault to be found with the one saving force in our moral situation—that extruded "high" segment of our general culture which, with its exigent, violently subversive spirituality, has the power of arming us against, and setting us apart from, all in the general culture that we hate and fear.

Then what justification can there be for describing with any degree of adversary purpose the diminished status of the principle of pleasure which characterizes this segment of our culture?

Possibly one small justification can be brought to light by reference to a famous passage in the *Confessions* of Saint Augustine, the one in which Augustine speaks of an episode of his adolescence and asks why he entered that orchard and stole those pears. Of all the acts of his unregenerate days which he calls sinful and examines in his grim, brilliant way, there is none that he nags so persistently, none that seems to lie so far beyond the reach of his ready comprehension of sin. He did not steal the pears because he was hungry. He did not steal them because they were delicious—they were pears of rather poor quality, he had better at home. He did not steal them to win the admiration of the friends who were with him, although this comes close, for, as he says, he would not have stolen them if he had been alone. In all sin, he says, there is a patent motivating desire, some good to be gained, some pleasure for the sake of which the act was committed. But this sin of the stolen pears is, as it were, pure—he can discover no human reason for it. He speaks again of the presence of the companions, but although their being with him was a necessary condition of the act, it cannot be said to have motivated it. To the mature Augustine, the petty theft of his youth is horrifying not only because it seems to have been a sin committed solely for the sake of sinning, but because, in having no conceivable pleasure in view, it was a sort of negative transcendence—in effect, a negation—of his humanity. This is not strange to us—what I have called the extruded high segment of our general culture has for

some time been engaged in an experiment in the negative transcendence of the human, a condition which is to be achieved by freeing
the self from its thralldom to pleasure. Augustine's puzzzling sin is
the paradigm of the modern spiritual enterprise, and in his reprobation of it is to be found the reason why Dostoevski contemned and
hated the Christianity of the West, which he denounced as, in effect,
a vulgar humanism.

To be aware of this undertaking of negative transcendence is,
surely, to admire the energy of its desperateness. And we can comprehend how, for the consumer of literature, for that highly developed person who must perforce live the bourgeois life in an affluent
society, an aesthetic ethos based on the devaluation of pleasure can
serve, and seem to save, one of the two souls which inhabit his
breast. Nearly overcome as we are by the specious good, insulted as
we are by being forced to acquire it, we claim the right of the
Underground Man to address the "gentlemen" with our assertion, "I
have more life in me than you have," which consorts better with the
refinement of our sensibility than other brags that men have made,
such as, "I am stronger than you," or "I am holier than thou." Our
high culture invites us to transfer our energies from the bourgeois
competition to the spiritual competition. We find our "distinction"—last or penultimate—in our triumph over the miserable "gentlemen," whether they are others or ourselves, whether our cry be, "I
have more life in me than you have" or "I have more life in me than
I have."

Now and then it must occur to us that the life of competition for
spiritual status is not without its own peculiar sordidness and absurdity. But this is a matter for the novelist—for that novelist we do
not yet have but must surely have one day, who will take into
serious and comic account the actualities of the spiritual career of
our time.

More immediately available to our awareness and more substantive and simple in itself is the effect which the devaluation of pleasure has upon the relation between our high literature and our life

in politics, taking that word in its largest possible sense. There was a time when literature assumed that the best ideals of politics were naturally in accord with its own essence, when poetry celebrated the qualities of social life which had their paradigmatic existence in poetry itself. Keats's *Poems* of 1817 takes for its epigraph two lines from Spenser which are intended to point up the political overtone of the volume: "What more felicity can fall to creature/Than to enjoy delight with liberty." Even when Wordsworth is deep in Toryism and Stoic Christianity, it is natural for him to assert the Utopian possibility.

> Paradise and groves
> Elysian, Fortunate Fields—like those of old
> Sought in the Atlantic Main—why should they be
> A history only of departed things,
> Or a mere fiction of what never was?

He goes on to say categorically that these imaginations may become, at the behest of rationality and good will, "a simple produce of the common day." But the old connection between literature and politics has been dissolved. For the typical modern literary personality, political life is likely to exist only as it makes an occasion for the disgust and rage which are essential to the state of modern spirituality, as one particular instance of the irrational, violent, and obscene fantasy which life in general is, as licensing the counter-fantasy of the poet.

In a recent essay,[9] William Phillips described in an accurate and telling way the division that has developed between modern literature and a rational and positive politics, and went on to explain why, for literature's sake, the separation must be maintained. "It now looks," Mr. Phillips said, "as though a radical literature and a radical politics must be kept apart. For radical politics of the modern variety has really served as an antidote to literature. The moral hygiene, the puritanism, the benevolence—all the virtues that sprout on the left—work like a cure for the perverse and morbid

---

[9] "What Happened in the 30's," *Commentary*, September 1962.

idealism of the modern writer. If writing is to be thought of as radical, it must be in a deeper sense, in the sense not simply of cutting across the grain of contemporary life but also of reaching for the connections between the real and the forbidden and the fantastic. The classic example is Dostoevski."

The situation that Mr. Phillips describes will scarcely be a matter of indifference to those of us who, while responding to the force of the perverse and morbid idealism of modern literature, are habituated to think of literature and politics as naturally having affinity with each other. We cannot but feel a discomfort of mind at the idea of their hostile separation, and we are led to ask whether the breach is as complete as Mr. Phillips says it is. His description, it seems to me, so far as it bears upon the situation of the moment, upon the situation as it presents itself to the practitioner of literature, needs no modification. But if we consider the matter in a more extended perspective, in the long view of the cultural historian, it must occur to us to speculate—even at the risk of being "hygienic"— whether the perverse and morbid idealism of modern literature is not to be thought of as being precisely political, whether it does not erpress a demand which in its own way is rational and positive and which may have to be taken into eventual account by a rational and positive politics.

If we do ask this question, we will be ready to remind ourselves that the devaluation of the pleasure principle, or, as perhaps we ought to put it, the imagination of going *beyond the pleasure principle* is, after all, not merely an event of a particular moment in culture. It is, as Freud made plain in his famous essay, a fact of the psychic life itself. The impulse to go beyond the pleasure principle is certainly to be observed not only in modern literature but in all literature, and of course not only in literature but in the emotional economy of at least some persons in all epochs. But what we can indeed call an event in culture is that at a particular moment in history, in our moment, this fact of the psychic life became a salient and dominant theme in literature, and also that it has been made explicit as a fact in the psychic life and forced upon our consciousness by Freud's momentous foray into metapsychology. And this cultural event may indeed be understood in political terms, as likely to have eventual political consequences, just as we understood in political terms and as having had political consequences the eighteenth-century assertion that the dignity of man was to be found in the principle of pleasure.

We deal with a change in quantity. It has always been true of some men that to pleasure they have preferred unpleasure. They imposed upon themselves difficult and painful tasks, they committed themselves to strange, "unnatural" modes of life, they sought out distressing emotions, in order to know psychic energies which are not to be summoned up in felicity. These psychic energies, even when they are experienced in self-destruction, are a means of self-definition and self-affirmation. As such, they have a social reference—the election of unpleasure, however isolate and private the act may be, must refer to society if only because the choice denies the valuation which society in general puts upon pleasure; and of course it often receives social approbation in the highest degree, even if at a remove of time: it is the choice of the hero, the saint and martyr, and, in some cultures, the artist. The quantitative change which we have to take account of is: what was once a mode of experience of a few has now become an ideal of experience of many. For reasons which, at least here, must defy speculation, the ideal of pleasure has exhausted itself, almost as if it had been actually realized and had issued in satiety and ennui. In its place, or, at least, beside it, there is developing—conceivably at the behest of literature!—an ideal of the experience of those psychic energies which are linked with unpleasure and which are directed toward self-definition and self-affirmation. Such an ideal makes a demand upon society for its satisfaction: it is a political fact. It surely asks for gratification of a sort which is not within the purview of ordinary democratic progressivism.

What I have called the spirituality of modern literature can scarcely be immune to irony, and the less so as we see it advancing in the easy comprehension of increasing numbers of people, to the point of its becoming, through the medium of the stage and the cinema, the stuff of popular entertainment—how can irony be withheld from an accredited subversiveness, an established moral radicalism, a respectable violence? But although the anomalies of the culture of the educated middle class do indeed justify an adversary response, and perhaps a weightier one than that of irony, a response that is nothing but adversary will not be adequate.

We often hear it said nowadays, usually by psychoanalysts and by writers oriented toward psychoanalysis, that the very existence of civilization is threatened unless society can give credence to the principle of pleasure and learn how to implement it. We understand what is meant, that repressiveness and oppression will be lessened if the principle of pleasure is established in our social arrangements, and we readily assent. Yet secretly we know that the formula does not satisfy the condition it addresses itself to—it leaves out of account those psychic energies which press beyond the pleasure principle and even deny it.

It is possible to say that—whether for good or for bad—we confront a mutation in culture by which an old established proportion between the pleasure-seeking instincts and the ego instincts is being altered in favor of the latter.[10] If we follow Freud through the awesome paradoxes of *Beyond the Pleasure Principle,* we may understand why the indications of this change should present themselves as perverse and morbid, for the other name that Freud uses for the ego instincts is the death instincts. Freud's having made the ego instincts synonymous with the death instincts accounts, more than anything else in his dark and difficult essay, for the cloud of misunderstanding in which it exists. But before we conclude that *Beyond the Pleasure Principle* issues, as many believe, in an ultimate

[10] See the remarks on tragedy in "On the Teaching of Modern Literature" (pp. 18 ff.) and also Lionel Abel's brilliant chapter on tragedy in *Metatheatre.* For a full and detailed account of the modern devaluation of that good fortune the destruction of which once pained us in tragedy, see Thomas Munro, "The Failure Story: A Study of Contemporary Pessimism," *The Journal of Aesthetics and Art Criticism,* Vol. XVII, No. 2, December 1958.

pessimism or "negation," and before we conclude that the tendencies in our literature which we have remarked on are nothing but perverse and morbid, let us recall that although Freud did indeed say that "the aim of all life is death," the course of his argument leads him to the statement that "the organism wishes to die only in its own fashion," only through the complex fullness of its appropriate life.

Freud: Within and Beyond Culture

I

THE profession of psychoanalysis is unique among modern professions in that it looks back to one man as its originator and founder. It has been said that this constitutes an intellectual disadvantage to the profession, that the great personality of Sigmund Freud is too much present and too decisive in the minds of those who come after him and thus stands in the way of their intellectual independence. My own sense of the matter is quite otherwise. I take it to be a clear advantage to any profession to have, as psychoanalysis does have, its whole history before its eyes, to be always conscious of the point in time at which it had its beginning, and of how its doctrines were devised, revised, and developed. To have this history in mind, made actual and dramatic in the person of Freud himself, must give the members of the profession a lively belief in intellectual possibility, and in the personal nature of cultural achievement, a wondering happy awareness of what a person can do toward the renovation of a culture.

In previous years the speakers on this anniversary have been psychoanalysts. This year you have interrupted that tradition and have invited your speaker from the profession of letters. He does not feel alien among you. Nowadays there is scarcely a humanistic discipline or a social science that has not been touched by Freud's ideas, and even theology feels the necessity of taking these ideas into account. Had you invited a philosopher as your speaker on this anniversary, or a historian, or an anthropologist, or a sociologist, or even a theologian, you would have acted with entire appropriateness and your guest would have had sufficient reason to feel at home among you. But of course no other profession has had so long or so intimate a connection with psychoanalysis as the profession of literature.

The important place that literature had in Freud's mental life and the strength of the feeling with which he regarded literature are well known. Dr. Ernst Kris, in his introduction to the letters which Freud wrote to Wilhelm Fliess, speaks of Freud's scientific interest as being "based on a firm foundation of the humanities." This is of course true, and it is one of the remarkable things about Freud. It is the more remarkable when we consider the nature of his scientific training, which was uncompromising in its materialism, and the force of the scientific ethos of his day, to which Freud himself enthusiastically subscribed.

We must, however, keep it in mind that only a relatively few years earlier in the nineteenth century it had not been at all remarkable to base one's scientific interests on the humanities. This earlier attitude is represented to us in a convenient and accurate way by the figure of Goethe. We all know what store Goethe set by his own scientific researches, and we know what part Goethe's famous essay on Nature played not only in the life of Freud but also in the lives of many other scientists of the century. Goethe, of course, was in the tradition of the *philosophes* and the Encyclopedists, who were preponderantly men of letters: the science of the late seventeenth century and the eighteenth century moved on a tide of literary enthusiasm and literary formulation.

Yet by the middle of the nineteenth century the separation between science and literature becomes complete, and an antagonism develops between them, and while it is indeed true that Freud based his scientific interests on the humanities, he was, above all else, a scientist. He was reared in the ethos of the nineteenth-century physical sciences, which was as rigorous and as jealous as a professional ethos can possibly be, and he found in that ethos the heroism which he always looked for in men, in groups, and in himself. He did not set out with the intention of becoming a humanist or of finding support for his scientific ideas in whatever authority humanism might have. And if, when we have examined his achievement, we cannot fail to pronounce him one of the very greatest of humanistic minds, we yet cannot say of him that he was in the least a literary mind.

A generation ago, literary men claimed Freud for their own, for reasons that are obvious enough, but nowadays it is not the tendency of literary men to continue this claim. The belief, which is now to be observed in some literary quarters, that Freud's science is hostile to the spirit of literature is as unconsidered a notion as the former belief that psychoanalysis was a sort of literary invention. Yet it is certainly true that, whatever natural affinity we see between Freud and literature, however great a contribution to the understanding of literature we judge him to have made, it must seem to a literary man that Freud sees literature not from within but from without. The great contribution he has made to our understanding of literature does not arise from what he says about literature itself but from what he says about the nature of the human mind: he showed us that poetry is indigenous to the very constitution of the mind; he saw the mind as being, in the greater part of its tendency, exactly a poetry-making faculty. When he speaks about literature itself, he is sometimes right and sometimes wrong. And sometimes, when he is wrong, his mistakes are more useful than literary men are willing to perceive. But he is always, I think, outside the process of literature. Much as he responds to the product, he does not really imagine the process. He does not have what we call the *feel* of the thing.

Freud was a scientist—this was the name he cherished and sought to deserve. Nowadays some of us have fallen into the habit of saying that there is no real difference between the mind of the scientist and the mind of the artist. We are all dismayed at the separateness and specialness of the disciplines of the mind, and when we meet together at conferences and round-tables designed to overcome this bad situation, we find it in our hearts to say to each other that we have everything in common, very little in difference. This is laudable in its motive, and no doubt it is true enough under some sufficiently large aspect. Yet in practical fact the difference is real and important, as of course we know. The reason I am insisting on the difference between the mind of the scientist and the mind of the literary man, and on Freud's being a scientist, is, obviously, that the recognition of this makes so much more interesting and significant the relation of Freud to humane letters.

The canon of Freud's work is large and complex, and the tradition of humane letters is patently not to be encompassed in any formulation of its nature. I must therefore be hopelessly crude and summary in an attempt to suggest the connection between the two. Literature is not a unitary thing, and there is probably no such single entity as *the* literary mind. But I shall assume that literature is what it actually is not, a unity, and I shall deal with it in those of its aspects in which that assumption does not immediately appear to be absurd, in which it is not wholly impossible to say that literature "is" or "does" this or that.

The first thing that occurs to me to say about literature, as I consider it in the relation in which Freud stands to it, is that literature is dedicated to the conception of the self. This is a very simple thing to say, perhaps to the point of dullness. But it becomes more complicated when we perceive how much of an achievement this conception is, how far it may be in advance of what society, or the general culture, can conceive. Tolstoi tells the story of the countess who wept buckets at a play while her coachman sat on the box of her waiting carriage, perishing of the cold through the long hours of the performance. This may stand for the discrepancy between what literature conceives of the self and what society, or the general culture, conceives. At the behest of literature, and with its help, the countess is able to imagine the selfhood of others, no doubt through the process of identification; she is not able, of herself, to imagine the selfhood of her own servant. What the *Iliad* conceives in the way of selfhood is far beyond what could be conceived by the culture in which it was written. *The Trojan Women* of Euripides must sometimes seem unendurable, so intense is the recognition of the selfhood of others in pain that it forces upon us. Yet it is possible that *The Trojan Women* was being composed at the very moment that Athens was infamously carrying out its reprisal against the city of Melos for wishing to remain neutral in the Peloponnesian War, slaughtering the men of the city and enslaving the women and children, doing this not in the passion of battle but, like the Greek princes of *The Trojan Women,* in the horrible deliberateness of policy. Thucydides understood the hideousness of the deed, and it is thought by some modern scholars that he conceived his *History* in the form of a tragedy in which the downfall of Athens is the consequence of her sin at Melos; but Thucydides does not record any party of opposition to the Melian decision or any revulsion among his fellow countrymen. In almost every developed society, literature is able to conceive of the self, and the selfhood of others, far more intensely than the general culture ever can.

One of the best-known tags of literary criticism is Coleridge's phrase, "the willing suspension of disbelief." Coleridge says that the willing suspension of disbelief constitutes "poetic faith." I suppose that we might say that it constitutes scientific faith too, or scientific method. Once we get beyond the notion that science is, as we used to be told it was, "organized common sense," and have come to understand that science is organized improbability, or organized fantasy, we begin to see that the willing suspension of disbelief is an essential part of scientific thought. And certainly the willing suspension of disbelief constitutes moral faith—the essence of the moral life would seem to consist in doing that most difficult thing in the world, making a willing suspension of disbelief in the selfhood of someone else. This Freud was able to do in a most extraordinary way, and not by the mere impulse of his temperament, but systematically, as an element of his science. We recall, for instance, that dramatic moment in the development of psychoanalysis when Freud accepted as literally true the stories told him by so many of his early patients, of their having been, as children, sexually seduced or assaulted by adults, often by their own parents. We know how his patients rewarded his credulity—scarcely any of them were telling the truth. They had betrayed Freud into constructing a hypothesis on the basis of their stories. Hypotheses are precious things and this one now had to be abandoned, and so Freud had reason to think very harshly of his patients if he wished to. But he did not blame them, he did not say they were lying—he willingly suspended his disbelief in their fantasies, which they themselves believed, and taught himself how to find the truth that was really in them.

It is hard to know whether to describe this incident as a triumph of the scientific imagination and its method or as the moral triumph of an impatient and even censorious man in whom the intention of therapy and discovery was stronger than the impulse to blame. But in whatever terms we choose to praise it, it has been established in the system of psychoanalytical therapy. From it followed the willing suspension of disbelief in the semantic value of dreams, and the willing suspension of disbelief in the concept of mind, which all well-trained neurologists and psychiatrists of Vienna knew to be but a chimera. Freud's acceptance of the fantasies of his early patients, his conclusion that their untruths had a meaning, a purpose, and even a value, was the suspension of disbelief in the selfhood of these patients. Its analogue is not, I think, the religious virtue of charity, but something in which the intelligence plays a greater part. We must be reminded of that particular kind of understanding, that particular exercise of the literary intelligence by which we judge adversely the deeds of Achilles, but not Achilles himself, by which we do not blame Macbeth, nor even, to mention the hero and heroine of Freud's favorite English poem, Adam and Eve, who, because they are the primal parents, we naturally want to blame for everything.

If we go on with our gross summary comparison of literature and psychoanalysis, we can say that they are also similar in this respect, that it is of the essence of both to represent the opposition between two principles, those which Freud called the reality principle and the pleasure principle. Whenever Freud goes wrong in his dealings with literature, it is because he judges literature by too limited an application of these principles. When he praises literature, it is chiefly because of its powers of factual representation, its powers of discovery—"Not I but the poets," he said, "discovered the unconscious." When he denigrates literature (by implication), it is by speaking of its mere hedonism, of its being an escape from reality, a substitute-gratification, a daydream, an anodyne. Some years ago I dealt as sternly as I could with the errors of these formulations of Freud's,[1] and so now perhaps I am privileged to lighten the burden of reprobation they have had to bear and to take note of a certain rightness and usefulness they have.

Freud is scarcely unique in conceiving of literature in terms of the opposition between reality and pleasure. This conception is endemic in literary criticism itself since at least the time of Plato, and often in a very simple form. It was usually in a very simple form indeed that the opposition was made in the nineteenth century. We have but to read the young Yeats and to observe his passion against fact and the literature of fact, and his avowed preference for the literature of dream, to see how established in the thought of the time was the opposition between the pleasure principle and the principle of reality.

Nowadays literary criticism tends to be restive under the opposition, which it takes to be a covert denial of the autonomy of literature, a way of judging literature by the categories of science. But the poets themselves have always accepted the opposition. They accept the commission to represent something called reality, which lies

[1] In "Freud and Literature," *The Liberal Imagination,* 1950.

outside of literature, and which they think of as either antagonistic to the dream of pleasure, or as standing beyond pleasure. Wordsworth blamed himself for having "lived in a dream," for having failed to represent to himself the painful adversity of the world. Keats denounced himself for his membership in the "tribe" of mere dreaming poets, who are so much less than "those to whom the miseries of the world/ Are misery, and will not let them rest."

> What benefit canst thou do, or all thy tribe,
> To the great world? Thou art a dreaming thing,
> A fever of thyself—think of the Earth . . .

Yet with the dream of pleasure, or with the actuality of pleasure, the poets, at least of an earlier time than ours, always kept in touch. Keats's whole mental life was an effort to demonstrate the continuity between pleasure and reality. Wordsworth speaks of the principle of pleasure—the phrase is his—as constituting the "naked and native dignity of man." He says, moreover, that it is the principle by which man not only "feels, and lives, and moves," but also "knows": the principle of pleasure was for Wordsworth the very ground of the principle of reality, and so of course it is for Freud, even though he seems to maintain the irreconcilability of the two principles. And the mature Yeats, in that famous sentence of his, which is as Freudian in its tendency as it is Wordsworthian, tells us that, "In dreams begins responsibility." He bases the developed moral life on the autonomy of the youthful hedonistic fantasies.

"Beauty is truth, truth beauty," said Keats, and generations of critics have been at pains to tell us that the equations are false. They forget what meaning we are required to assign to the two predications by reason of the fact that Keats utters them in the context of a passionate meditation on four great facts of human existence—love, death, art, and the relation that exists among these. When Keats said that beauty is truth, he was saying that the pleasure principle is at the root of existence, and of knowledge, and of the moral life. When he said that truth is beauty, he was putting in two words his enormously complex belief that the self can so develop that it may, in the intensity of art or meditation, perceive even very painful facts with a kind of pleasure, for it is one of the striking things about Keats that he represents so boldly and accurately the development of the self, and that, when he speaks of pleasure, he may mean—to use a language not his—sometimes the pleasure of the id, sometimes of the ego, and sometimes of the superego.

Keats's mind was profoundly engaged by the paradox of the literary genre of tragedy, which must always puzzle us because it seems to propose to the self a gratification in regarding its own extinction. Very eminent psychoanalysts, continuators of Freud's science who would perhaps differ with him on no other point, do differ with him on the matter of his having conceived a tendency of the self to acquiesce in and even to desire its own end. Whether or not Freud's formulations of the death instinct stand up under scientific inquiry, I of course cannot venture to say. But certainly they confirm our sense of Freud's oneness with the tradition of literature. For literature has always recorded an impulse of the self to find affirmation even in its own extinction, even *by* its own extinction. When we read the great scene of the death of Oedipus at Colonus, we have little trouble, I think, in at least suspending our disbelief in Freud's idea. We do so the more willingly because the impulse to death is, in this magnificent moment, expressed and exemplified by the most passionate of men, the man in whom the energy of will and intellect was greatest, the man, too, who at the moment of his desire for death speaks of his extraordinary power of love. It is possible to argue that Oedipus does not in fact go to his death but to his apotheosis. It is possible, too, to say that when the poets speak of the desire for death or the happy acquiescence in death, they do not really mean death at all but apotheosis, or Nirvana, or what Yeats imagined, the existence "out of nature," in the "artifice of eternity." It is possible to say that something of this sort is really what Freud meant. But the poets call it death; it has much of the aspect of death; and when we take into account the age-old impulse of highly developed spirits to incorporate the idea of death into the experience of life, even to make death the criterion of life, we are drawn to the belief that the assertion of the death instinct is the effort of finely tempered minds to affirm the self in an ultimate confrontation of reality.

There is yet another theme with which literature and Freud have an equal preoccupation. It is again a theme of opposition, cognate with the opposition between pleasure and reality—the theme of the opposition between love and power. That literature does conceive love and power as being in opposition is obvious enough from the frequency with which it presents the hero as both lover and warrior, the interest of his situation being that he finds it very hard to reconcile his desire for love and his desire for power. The theme has engaged not only the dramatic poets and the novelists but the lyric poets too—it was a lyric poet who put so large a part of the matter in a nutshell: "I could not love thee (Deare) so much,/ Lov'd I not Honour more," for the power I speak of is not gross, cruel power (although, in the context, this cannot be far from our minds) but rather, in its ideal conception, what is represented by the word *honor:* it is the power of cultural achievement, or of cultural commitment. As such, it was seen by Freud as pre-eminently a masculine issue. "The masculine character, the ability to dare and endure, to know and not to fear reality, to look the world in the face and take it for what it is, . . . this is what I want to preserve." It is not Freud I am quoting but one of Henry James's heroes, an American; but Basil Ransom of *The Bostonians* says very well what Freud meant. And Freud's concern for the preservation of what James calls "the masculine character," which, like James, Freud conceived to be under attack, has been made a point in the reproach directed at Freud that he displayed a masculine chauvinism, and, what is more, that, for all his overt preoccupation with love, he was yet more preoccupied with power, with aggression and personal force, or, at the best, with achievement. This contributes to a tendency which is to be observed of recent years, the tendency to represent Freud as really anesthetic to love and as in some way antagonistic to it. We all know how it has been said of Freud that he has made out love to be nothing but a reaction-formation against the most selfish and hostile impulses. And so strange are the surprises of the movement of thought that Freud, once attacked for the extravagance of his sexual emphasis, is now, by people of no little seriousness, said to be puritanical in his view of sexuality, surrendering to civilization and to achievement in civilization far more of impulse than there was any need to surrender.

This is not a matter that can be argued here. I should like only to turn again to literature and to observe that the tendency of literature, when once it has represented the opposition between love and power, is to conceive of love as a principle of order for the self, even as a discipline, and as itself a power, a civic and civilizing power. Oedipus, that angry and violent man who pauses in his dying to set the word *love* at the very heart of experience, saying of himself, as Yeats translates the speech, "No living man has loved as I have loved," becomes the guardian genius of the Athenian civic life. William Blake, who envisaged life in a way that Freud would have easily understood, calls in a great voice, "Bring me my bow of burning gold!/ Bring me my arrows of desire./ Bring me my spear! . . ." What does he want this libidinal armament for? Why, that he "may build Jerusalem/ In England's green and pleasant land." And in his fine poem on the death of Freud, W. H. Auden speaks of the grief both of "anarchic Aphrodite" and of "Eros, builder of cities."

Freud was much concerned with his own cultural commitment and achievement. And he loved fame. To some it may be surprising and even dismaying that this should be said of him; they will suppose that it does him no credit. In our culture the love of fame is not considered a virtue, or even an attractive trait of the personality. We are likely to confuse it with the love of publicity, and thus to be confirmed in our feeling that it is not a worthy motive of intellectual ambition. It is, I believe, considered particularly unbecoming in a scientist. But it is a trait which confirms our sense of Freud's personal connection with the tradition of literature, and my mention of it is meant as praise. Traditionally the love of fame has characterized two highly regarded professions, that of arms and that of letters. The soldier, however, is no longer supposed to desire fame. And even the poet, although I think we license him to entertain the fantasy of his immortal renown, no longer praises fame or says he wants it, as once he thought it very proper to do. Dante desired above all earthly things to be famous as a poet. Shakespeare believed implicitly in the permanence of his fame. Milton calls the love of fame "that last infirmity of noble mind," but he thus connects it with mind; and he speaks of it as an ally of the reality principle:

> Fame is the spur that the *clear* spirit doth raise
> To scorn delights and live laborious days.

There can be no doubt that fame was the spur to Freud's clear spirit, to his desire to make clear what was darkly seen. As a student he stood in the great Aula of the University of Vienna, where were set up the busts of the famous men of the University, and he dreamed of the day when he should be similarly honored. He knew exactly what inscription he wanted on the pedestal, a line from *Oedipus Tyrannus,* "Who divined the riddle of the Sphinx and was a man most mighty"—the story is told by his biographer that he turned pale, as if he had seen a ghost, when, on his fiftieth birthday, he was presented by his friends and admirers with a medallion on which these very words were inscribed.

And if we ask what moves the poets to their love of fame, what made the dying Keats say in despair, "Here lies one whose name is writ in water," and then again in hope, "I think I shall be among the English poets," the answer is not so very difficult to come by. The poets' idea of fame is the intense expression of the sense of the self, of the self defined by the thing it makes, which is conceived to be everlasting precisely because it was once a new thing, a thing added to the spirit of man.

II

Literature offers itself to our understanding in many ways. Of these not the least important is that which takes literature to be an intellectual discipline having to do with appearance and reality, with truth. The truth we especially expect literature to convey to us by its multifarious modes of communication is the truth of the self, and also the truth about the self, about the conditions of its existence, its survival, its development. For literature, as for Freud, the self is the first object of attention and solicitude. The culture in which the self has its existence is a matter of the liveliest curiosity, but in a secondary way, as an essential condition of the self, as a chief object of the self's energies, or as representing the aggregation of selves. For literature, as for Freud, the test of the culture is always the individual self, not the other way around. The function of literature, through all its mutations, has been to make us aware of the particularity of selves, and the high authority of the self in its quarrel with its society and its culture. Literature is in that sense subversive. This is not to say that the general culture does not have its own kind of awareness of the self. It does; it must—and when we judge a culture we inevitably adduce the way it conceives of the self, the value and honor it gives to the self. But it can sometimes happen that a culture intent upon giving the very highest value and honor to the selves that comprise it can proceed on its generous enterprise without an accurate awareness of what the self is, or what it might become. Such a loss of accurate knowledge about the self it is possible to observe in our own culture at this time. It is, I believe, a very generous culture, and in its conscious thought it sets great store by the conditions of life which are manifestly appropriate to the self, the conditions of freedom and respect. Yet it would seem that this generosity of intention does not preclude a misapprehension of the nature of the self, and of the right relation of the self to the culture. What I take to be a progressive deterioration of accurate knowledge of the self and of the right relation between the self and the culture is rationalized by theories and formulas to which Freud's thought about the self and the culture stands as a challenge and a controversion.

The idea of culture, in the modern sense of the word, is a relatively new idea. It represents a way of thinking about our life in society which developed concomitantly with certain new ways of conceiving of the self. Indeed, our modern idea of culture may be thought of as a new sort of selfhood bestowed upon the whole of society. The idea of society as a person is not new, but there is much that is new about the kind of personalization of society which began to be made some two hundred years ago. Society, in this new selfhood, is thought of as having a certain organic unity, an autonomous character and personality which it expresses in everything it does; it is conceived to have a *style,* which is manifest not only in its conscious, intentional activities, in its architecture, its philosophy, and so on, but also in its unconscious activities, in its unexpressed assumptions—the unconscious of society may be said to have been imagined before the unconscious of the individual. And in the degree that society was personalized by the concept of culture, the individual was seen to be far more deeply implicated in society than ever before. This is not an idea which is confined to the historian or to the social scientist; it is an idea which is at work in the mind of every literate and conscious person as he thinks of his life and estimates the chances of his living well in the world. At some point in the history of the West—let us say, for convenience, at the time of Rousseau—men began to think of their fates as being lived out in relation not to God, or to the individual persons who are their neighbors, or to material circumstance, but to the ideas and assumptions and manners of a large social totality. The evidence of this is to be found in our literature, in its preoccupation with newly discovered alien cultures which, in one regard or another, serve to criticize our own. Walter Scott could not have delighted the world with his representation in *Waverley* of the loyalty, sincerity, and simplicity of the Highland clans had not the world learned to think of life in terms of culture, had it not learned to wonder whether some inscrutable bad principle in its present culture was not making it impossible for all men to be as loyal and sincere and simple as they should be.

In the dissemination of the idea of culture, Freud has no doubt had a chief part. The status of Freud's actual formulations about culture is now somewhat ambiguous. We often hear it said that Freud's theories of culture are inadequate. It seems to me that this is often said by writers on the subject just before they make use of some one of Freud's ideas about culture. But whatever we may conclude about the intellectual value of Freud's formulations, we cannot fail to know that it was Freud who made the idea of culture real for a great many of us. Whatever he may mean to the people who deal professionally with the idea of culture—and in point of fact he means a great deal—for the layman Freud is likely to be the chief proponent of the whole cultural concept. It was he who made it apparent to us how entirely implicated in culture we all are. By what he said or suggested of the depth and subtlety of the influence of the family upon the individual, he made plain how the culture suffuses the remotest parts of the individual mind, being taken in almost literally with the mother's milk. His psychology involves culture in its very essence—it tells us that the surrogates of culture are established in the mind itself, that the development of the individual mind recapitulates the development of culture.

Generally speaking, the word *culture* is used in a sense which approaches the honorific. When we look at a people in the degree of abstraction which the idea of culture implies, we cannot but be touched and impressed by what we see, we cannot help being awed by something mysterious at work, some creative power which seems to transcend any particular act or habit or quality that may be observed. To make a coherent life, to confront the terrors of the outer and the inner world, to establish the ritual and art, the pieties and duties which make possible the life of the group and the indi-

vidual—these are culture, and to contemplate these various enterprises which constitute a culture is inevitably moving. And, indeed,
without this sympathy and admiration a culture is a closed book to
the student, for the scientific attitude requisite for the study of cultures is based on a very lively subjectivity. It is not merely that the
student of culture must make a willing suspension of disbelief in the
assumptions of cultures other than his own; he must go even further and feel that the culture he has under examination is somehow
justified, that it is as it should be.

This methodological sympathy, as we might call it, developed into
a kind of principle of cultural autonomy, according to which cultures were to be thought of as self-contained systems not open to
criticism from without; and this principle was taken from the anthropologists by certain psychoanalysts. In this view a culture became a kind of absolute. The culture was not to be judged "bad" or
"neurotic"; it was the individual who was to be judged by the
criteria of the culture. This view, I believe, no longer obtains in its
old force. We are no longer forbidden to judge cultures adversely;
we may now speak of them as inadequate cultures, even as downright neurotic cultures. And yet the feeling for the absoluteness of
culture still persists. It may best be observed in our responses to the
cultures we think of as having a "folk" character and in our tendency to suppose that when an individual is at one with a culture of
this sort he is in a happy and desirable state of existence. This will
suggest the unconscious use we make of the idea of culture: we take
it to be a useful and powerful support to the idea of *community,* for
what we respond to in a folk culture is what we see, or seem to see,
of the unity and coherence of its individual members, the absence of
conflict, the sense of the wholeness of the group.

But Freud's attitude to culture is different from this. For him, too,
there is an honorific accent in the use of the word, but at the same
time, as we cannot fail to hear, there is in what he says about culture
an unfailing note of exasperation and resistance. Freud's relation to
culture must be described as an ambivalent one.

Recently, in another connection, I spoke of the modern self as characterized by its intense and adverse imagination of the culture in which it had its being, and by certain powers of indignant perception which, turned upon the unconscious portions of culture, have made them accessible to conscious thought.[2] Freud's view of culture is marked by this *adverse* awareness, by this indignant perception. He does indeed see the self as formed by its culture. But he also sees the self as set against the culture, struggling against it, having been from the first reluctant to enter it. Freud would have understood what Hegel meant by speaking of the *"terrible* principle of culture." This resistance, this tragic regret over the necessary involvement with culture, is obviously not the sole or even the dominant element in Freud's thought on the subject. Freud was, as he said of himself, a conservative, a conserving, mind. The aim of all his effort is the service of culture—he speaks of the work of psychoanalysis as "the draining of the Zuyder Zee," the building of the dyke, the seeing to it that where id was ego should be. Yet at the same time his adverse attitude to culture is very strong, his indignation is very intense.

It can of course be said that the indignation which an individual directs upon his culture is itself culturally conditioned. Culture may be thought of as Kismet—we flee from Bokhara to escape its decrees, only to fulfill them in Samarra. Yet the illusion, if that is what it be, of separateness from one's culture has an effect upon conduct, and upon culture, which is as decisive as the effects of the illusion of free will. For Freud this separateness was a necessary belief. He needed to believe that there was some point at which it was possible to stand beyond the reach of culture. Perhaps his formulation of the death-instinct is to be interpreted as the expression of this need. "Death destroys a man," says E. M. Forster, "but the idea of death saves him." Saves him from what? From the entire submission of himself—of his self—to life in culture.

At this point you will perhaps be wondering why I said that Freud so greatly influenced our idea of culture, for certainly this

---

[2] The reference is to a passage in the Preface to *The Opposing Self*, 1955.

aspect of Freud—his resistance to culture—is not reflected in our present-day thought. We set so much store by the idea of man in culture because, as I say, we set so much store (and rightly) by the idea of man in community. The two ideas are not the same. But the idea of man-in-culture provides, as it were, the metaphysic, the mystique, of our ideas of man-in-community. It gives us a way of speaking more profoundly about community, for talking about souls, about destiny, about the ground and sanctions of morality; it is our way of talking about fate, free will, and immortality. It is our way of coming close to the idea of Providence. I of course do not mean that we do not criticize our culture as it actually is. Indeed, nothing is more characteristic of our thinking today than our readiness to observe certain obvious failings and inadequacies of our cultural situation. Yet in every criticism that we utter, we express our belief that man can be truly himself and fully human only if he is in accord with his cultural environment, and, also, only if the cultural environment is in accord with the best tendencies in himself. This idea is not specifically a Freudian idea. It is the idea, or the assumption, on which the tradition of humane liberal thought has gone about its business for two centuries. But although it was not in the first instance derived from Freud, it is confirmed by the tendency of certain Freudian ideas. And it may be said to constitute a chief ground of our theories of education, child rearing, morality, and social action.

But if we speak of the Freudianism which supports so much of our current doctrine, we must also speak of our anti-Freudianism. An ambivalent attitude toward Freudianism is perhaps inevitable and maybe even healthy. But I do not have in mind what might be called the normal ambivalence of response to Freud's ideas. Rather, I speak of the particular resentment—for such it can be called—of Freud's theories of the self in its relation to culture. What I have described of Freud's tragic sense of culture, of his apparent wish to establish the self beyond the reach of culture, will suggest the ground for this hostility. For the fact is that Freud challenges our sense of how the self relates to culture and of how it should relate to culture. He shakes us most uncomfortably in those very ideas which we believe we have learned from him.

Several years ago, in the period of McCarthyism, a conference of notable American psychiatrists was convened for the purpose of discovering whether, and to what extent, the psychic health of the nation was affected by the requirement that people in civic positions take loyalty oaths and submit to the investigation of their ideas, attitudes, and past associations.[3] The consensus of the conference was that the atmosphere of surveillance and repressiveness must inevitably have an adverse effect upon psychic health generally. It was not merely said that individuals were being made anxious by the institutionalized suspiciousness to which they were being subjected or that the threat to their jobs and to their social acceptability made them fearful, and that fear made them cautious and secretive. The effect was said to be of a far deeper kind, and likely to perpetuate itself in the culture. The psychiatrists pointed out that the ego is that aspect of the mind which deals with the object-world, and that one of its important functions is the pleasurable entertainment of the ideal of adventure. But if part of the object-world is closed off by interdiction, and if the impulse to adventure is checked by restriction, the free functioning of the ego is impaired. The superego is also liable to serious damage. The psychiatrists of the conference said that "a mature superego can optimally develop only in a free and democratic society."

Now obviously there is much in this that no one will disagree with. What the conference says in the language of psychiatry, we all say in our own language. If you enslave a man, he will develop the psychology of a slave. If you exclude a man from free access to the benefits of society, his human quality will be in some way diminished. All men of good intention are likely to say something of this kind as they think of social betterment.

And yet if we look critically at these ideas, they will be seen not to

3 "Considerations Regarding the Loyalty Oath as a Manifestation of Current Social Tension and Anxiety: A Statement Formulated by the Committee on Social Issues of the Group for the Advancement of Psychiatry and a Panel Discussion." G.A.P. Symposium No. 1, Topeka, Kansas, October 1954.

go so far along the way to truth as at first we think. What, to take a relevant example, was the cultural and political situation in which Freud's thought developed, and his ego and his superego too? Dr. Jones tells us something about this in the first volume of his biography of Freud, but I shall draw my answer from the report of an American writer whom Freud particularly admired. Mark Twain lived in Vienna at the time Freud was formulating his theory of psychoanalysis; he attended many of the sessions of the Parliament of 1897 and he described some of them. One event, which especially horrified him, was the Parliament's surrender of its own authority, for it invited a militarized police force to march into the House to remove certain unruly members. Mark Twain certainly had no high opinion of the manners of American legislators, but he was appalled by what he observed in the Viennese Parliament, the show of personal violence, the personal invective of the rudest and most obscene sort. "As to the make-up of the House itself," he said, "it is this: the deputies come from all the walks of life and from all the grades of society. There are princes, counts, barons, priests, mechanics, laborers, lawyers, physicians, professors, merchants, bankers, shopkeepers. They are religious men, they are earnest, sincere, devoted, and they hate the Jews." This hatred of the Jews was the one point of unity in a Parliament which was torn asunder by the fiercest nationalistic and cultural jealousies. And the weakness of Parliament meant the strength of the monarchical government, which ruled by police methods; censorship was in force, and only inefficiency kept it from being something graver than a nuisance.

Of course no one who knows the circumstances of Freud's life will conclude that he lived under actual oppression in Vienna. Still, it was anything but a free and democratic society as the conference of psychiatrists, or most of us, would define a free and democratic society, and Freud was not an enfranchised citizen of it until his middle years. His having been reared in such a society surely goes far to explain why some of his views of culture are tragic or skeptical, and very far toward explaining why he conceived of the self as standing in opposition to the general culture. But the cultural circumstance in which he was reared did not, so far as I can make out, impair the functioning of his ego or his superego.

Why did it not? Well, certain things in his particular cultural situation intervened between him and the influence of his society. His family situation, for one thing: the family is the conduit of cultural influences, but it is also a bulwark against cultural influences. His ethnic situation, for another thing: he was a Jew, and enough of the Jewish sub-culture reached him to make a countervailing force against the general culture. Then his education: who can say what part in his self-respect, in his ability to move to a point beyond the reach of the surrounding dominant culture, was played by the old classical education, with its image of *the other culture,* the ideal culture, that wonderful imagined culture of the ancient world which no one but schoolboys, schoolmasters, scholars, and poets believed in? The schoolboy who kept his diary in Greek, as Freud did, was not submitting his ego or his superego to the debilitating influences of a restrictive society. Then the culture of another nation intervened between him and what was bad in his own culture: Freud's early love of England must be counted among his defenses. Then he found strength in certain aspects of his own culture, bad as it may have been by our standards of freedom and democracy: he loved the language and thus made it his friend, and he loved science.

And then beyond these cultural interpositions there was his sense of himself as a biological fact. This sense of himself as a biological fact was of course supported and confirmed by the various accidents of Freud's cultural fate, but it was, to begin with, a *given,* a *donnée* —a gift. It was a particular quantity and a particular quality of human energy, and its name was Sigmund Freud.

The place of biology in Freud's system of thought has often been commented on, and generally adversely. It is often spoken of as if it represented a reactionary part of Freud's thought. The argument takes this form: if we think of a man as being conditioned not so much by biology as by culture, we can the more easily envisage a beneficent manipulation of his condition; if we keep our eyes fixed upon the wide differences among cultures which may be observed, and if we repudiate Freud's naïve belief that there is a human *given* in all persons and all cultures, then we are indeed encouraged to think that we can do what we wish with ourselves, with mankind— there is no beneficent mutation of culture, there is no revision of the nature of man, that we cannot hope to bring about.

Now Freud may be right or he may be wrong in the place he gives to biology in human fate, but I think we must stop to consider whether this emphasis on biology, correct or incorrect, is not so far from being a reactionary idea that it is actually a liberating idea. It proposes to us that culture is not all-powerful. It suggests that there is a residue of human quality beyond the reach of cultural control, and that this residue of human quality, elemental as it may be, serves to bring culture itself under criticism and keeps it from being absolute.

This consideration is, I believe, of great importance to us at this moment in our history. The argument I made from Freud's own cultural situation in boyhood was, as I know, in some degree unfair, for the society of Vienna, although certainly not what we would call free and democratic, was apparently such a mess of a society that one might, without difficulty, escape whatever bad intentions it had; and its tolerance of mess may lead us to conclude that it had certain genial intentions of freedom. Nowadays, however, societies are less likely to be messes; they are likely to be all too efficient, whether by coerciveness or seductiveness. In a society like ours, which, despite some appearances to the contrary, tends to be seductive rather than coercive, the individual's old defenses against the domination of the culture become weaker and weaker. The influence of the family deteriorates and is replaced by the influence of the school. The small separatist group set apart by religious or ethnic difference loses its authority, or uses what authority it has to support the general culture. The image of what I have called *the other culture,* the ideal-ized past of some other nation, Greece, or Rome, or England, is dismissed from education at the behest of the pedagogic sense of reality—it is worth noting that, for perhaps the first time in history, the pedagogue is believed to have a sense of reality. And we have come to understand that it is not a low Philistine impulse that leads us to scrutinize with anxiety our children's success in their social life; it is rather a frank, free, generous, democratic, progressive awareness of the charms of Group-Living, an engaging trust in the natural happiness of man-in-culture, or child-in-culture, so long as that culture is not overtly hostile.

We do not need to have a very profound quarrel with American culture to feel uneasy because our defenses against it, our modes of escape from it, are becoming less and less adequate. We can scarcely fail to recognize how open and available to the general culture the individual becomes, how little protected he is by countervailing cultural forces, how the national culture grows in homogeneity and demandingness, even in those of its aspects that we think of as most free and benign. And if we do recognize this, we can begin to see why we may think of Freud's emphasis on biology as being a liberating idea. It is a resistance to and a modification of the cultural omnipotence. We reflect that somewhere in the child, somewhere in the adult, there is a hard, irreducible, stubborn core of biological urgency, and biological necessity, and biological *reason,* that culture cannot reach and that reserves the right, which sooner or later it will exercise, to judge the culture and resist and revise it. It seems to me that whenever we become aware of how entirely we are involved in our culture and how entirely controlled by it we believe ourselves to be, destined and fated and foreordained by it, there must come to us a certain sense of liberation when we remember our biological selves. In her lecture of 1954 before this Society and Institute, Anna Freud spoke of what she called the period of optimism in the psychoanalytical thought about the rearing of children, a period when, as she says, "almost the whole blame for the neurotic development of the child was laid on parental actions" and when "it was hoped that the modification of these parental attitudes would do away with infantile anxiety and, consequently, abolish the infantile neuroses." And Miss Freud went on to speak of the following "period of pessimism, when the origin of neurosis was recognized to be due not to environmental influences but to inevitable factors of various kinds." Pessimistic this new period of psychoanalytical thought may be; yet when we think of the growing power of culture to control us by seduction or coercion, we must be glad and not sorry that some part of our fate comes from outside the culture.

We must not permit ourselves to be at the mercy of the terrible pendulum of thought and begin now to discredit all that we have learned about cultural influence or conclude that parents have been suddenly relieved of all responsibility for their children's psychic destinies. Yet this new emphasis, of which Miss Freud speaks, upon the non-cultural part of our destiny may well serve to renovate and freshen our mode of thinking about ourselves.

The interaction of biology and culture in the fate of man is not a matter which we have yet begun to understand. Up to now, entranced by all that the idea of culture and the study of culture can tell us about the nature of man, we have been inclined to assign to culture an almost exclusive part in man's fate. If the culture goes awry, we say, inevitably the individual goes awry—his ego and his superego suffer serious impairment. But history does not always support this view. Sometimes it does, but not always. It is sometimes to be observed that a whole people will degenerate because of a drastic change in its economic and political and thus of its cultural situation. But then too, it sometimes happens that a people living under imposed conditions of a very bad kind, the opposite of the conditions of that free and democratic society which the ego and the superego are said to need for health and maturity, living, indeed, under persecution, will develop egos and superegos of an amazing health and strength. Whether also of maturity I will not venture to say, for maturity is a difficult word to comprehend, and even should we succeed in knowing what it imports, we might be hard put to carry its meaning from one culture to another: but strength and health they certainly have, enough to make for survival on a high cultural level. They have their psychic casualties, their psychic scars are manifest, but they survive in sufficient dignity. And if we ask why they thus survived, the answer may be that they conceived of their egos and superegos as not being culturally conditioned and dependent but as being virtually biological facts, and immutable. And often they put this conception of their psyches to the ultimate biological test—they died for the immutability of their egos and superegos.

What, to shift our ground from the group to the individuals, made it possible for a Giordano Bruno, or a Socrates, or any other martyr of the intellect, to face his death? It was not, I think, that a free and democratic society had successfully nurtured the maturity of his superego. How very strange is the superego! For we say of it that it is the surrogate of society, or of the culture, but one of its functions seems to be to lead us to imagine that there is a sanction beyond the culture, that there is a place from which the culture may be judged and rejected. It often happens that culture is very grateful for being so judged and rejected, that it gives the highest reminiscent honors to those who have escaped it. But we make it that much harder to escape the culture, we cut off the possibility of those triumphs of the mind that are won in the face of culture, if we impose the idea of a self that is wholly dependent upon the culture for its energy and health.

"Suppose," I heard a student on my own campus say the other day, "suppose a man is paranoid—that is, he thinks he is right and other people are wrong." He did not really, or he did not wholly, mean what he said—had he been questioned, he would have owned to a lively and reasoned admiration for the long tradition of the men who thought they were right and everybody else was wrong, he would have happily admitted that this isolation in belief was not only a sign of insanity. But at the moment at which he made his utterance he was speaking with the voice of the tendency of his culture. He was not one of the group of my own students who, a short time ago, read with me Freud's *Civilization and Its Discontents,* but he was kin to them, for they told me that Freud had presented a paranoid version of the relation of the self to culture: he conceived of the self submitting to culture and being yet in opposition to it; he conceived of the self as being not wholly continuous with culture, as being not wholly created by culture, as maintaining a standing quarrel with its great benefactor.

I need scarcely remind you that in respect of this "paranoia" Freud is quite at one with literature. In its essence literature is concerned with the self; and the particular concern of the literature of the last two centuries has been with the self in its standing quarrel with culture. We cannot mention the name of any great writer of the modern period whose work has not in some way, and usually in a passionate and explicit way, insisted on this quarrel, who has not expressed the bitterness of his discontent with civilization, who has not said that the self made greater legitimate demands than any culture could hope to satisfy. This intense conviction of the existence of the self apart from culture is, as culture well knows, its noblest and most generous achievement. At the present moment it must be thought of as a liberating idea without which our developing ideal of community is bound to defeat itself. We can speak no greater praise of Freud than to say that he placed this idea at the very center of his thought.

Isaac Babel

A GOOD many years ago, in 1929, I chanced to read a book which disturbed me in a way I can still remember. The book was called *Red Cavalry;* it was a collection of stories about Soviet regiments of horse operating in Poland. I had never heard of the author, Isaac Babel—or I. Babel as he signed himself—and nobody had anything to tell me about him, and part of my disturbance was the natural shock we feel when, suddenly and without warning, we confront a new talent of great energy and boldness. But the book was disturbing for other reasons as well.

In those days one still spoke of the "Russian experiment" and one might still believe that the light of dawn glowed on the test-tubes and crucibles of human destiny. And it was still possible to have very strange expectations of the new culture that would arise from the Revolution. I do not remember what my own particular expectations were, except that they involved a desire for an art that would have as little ambiguity as a proposition in logic. Why I wanted this I don't wholly understand. It was as if I had hoped that the literature of the Revolution would realize some simple, inadequate notion of the "classical" which I had picked up at college; and perhaps I was drawn to this notion of the classical because I was afraid of the literature of modern Europe, because I was scared of its terrible intensities, ironies, and ambiguities. If this is what I really felt, I can't say that I am now wholly ashamed of my cowardice. If we stop to think of the museum knowingness about art which we are likely to acquire with maturity, of our consumer's pride in buying only the very best spiritual commodities, the ones which are sure to give satisfaction, there may possibly be a grace in those moments when we lack the courage to confront, or the strength to endure, some particular work of art or kind of art. At any rate, here was Babel's book and I found it disturbing. It was obviously the most remarkable work of fiction that had yet come out of revolutionary Russia, the only work, indeed, that I knew of as having upon it the mark of exceptional talent, even of genius. Yet for me it was all too heavily charged with the intensity, irony, and ambiguousness from which I wished to escape.

There was anomaly at the very heart of the book, for the Red cavalry of the title were Cossack regiments, and why were Cossacks fighting for the Revolution, they who were the instrument and symbol of Czarist repression? The author, who represented himself in the stories, was a Jew; and a Jew in a Cossack regiment was more than an anomaly, it was a joke, for between Cossack and Jew there existed not merely hatred but a polar opposition. Yet here was a Jew riding as a Cossack and trying to come to terms with the Cossack ethos. The stories were about violence of the most extreme kind, yet they were composed with a striking elegance and precision of objectivity, and also with a kind of lyric *joy,* so that one could not at once know just how the author was responding to the brutality he recorded, whether he thought it good or bad, justified or not justified. Nor was this the only thing to be in doubt about. It was not really clear how the author felt about, say, Jews; or about religion; or about the goodness of man. He had—or perhaps, for the sake of some artistic effect, he pretended to have—a secret. This alienated and disturbed me. It was impossible not to be overcome by admiration for *Red Cavalry,* but it was not at all the sort of book that I had wanted the culture of the Revolution to give me.

And, as it soon turned out, it was not at all the sort of book that the Revolution wanted to give anyone. No event in the history of Soviet culture is more significant than the career, or, rather, the end of the career, of Isaac Babel. He had been a protégé of Gorki, and he had begun his career under the aegis of Trotsky's superb contempt for the pieties of the conventional "proletarian" aesthetics. In the last years of the decade of the twenties and in the early thirties he was regarded as one of the most notable talents of Soviet literature. This judgment was, however, by no means an official one. From the beginning of his career, Babel had been under the attack of the literary bureaucracy. But in 1932 the Party abolished RAPP—the Russian Association of Proletarian Writers—and it seemed that a new period of freedom had been inaugurated. In point of fact, the reactionary elements of Soviet culture were established in full ascendancy, and the purge trials of 1937 were to demonstrate how absolute their power was. But in the five intervening years the Party chose to exercise its authority in a lenient manner. It was in this atmosphere of seeming liberality that the first Writers' Congress was held in 1934. Babel was one of the speakers at the Congress. He spoke with considerable jauntiness, yet he spoke as a penitent—the stories he had written since *Red Cavalry* had been published in a volume at the end of 1932 and since that time he had written nothing, he had disappointed expectation.

His speech was a strange performance.[1] It undertook to be humorous; the published report is punctuated by indications of laughter. It made the avowals of loyalty that were by then routine, yet we cannot take it for granted that Babel was insincere when he spoke of his devotion to the Revolution, to the government, and to the state, or when he said that in a bourgeois country it would inevitably have been his fate to go without recognition and livelihood. And perhaps he was sincere even when he praised Stalin's literary style, speaking of the sentences "forged" as if of steel, of the necessity of learning to work in language as Stalin did. Yet beneath the orthodoxy of this speech there lies some hidden intention. One

[1] I am indebted to Professor Rufus Mathewson for the oral translation of Babel's speech which he made for me. Professor Mathewson was kindness itself in helping me to information about Babel; he is, of course, not accountable for any inaccuracy or awkwardness that may appear in my use of the facts.

feels this in the sad vestiges of the humanistic mode that wryly manifest themselves. It is as if the humor, which is often of a whimsical kind, as if the irony and the studied self-depreciation, were forlorn affirmations of freedom and selfhood; it is as if Babel were addressing his fellow writers in a dead language, or in some slang of their student days, which a few of them might perhaps remember.

Everything, he said at one point in his speech, is given to us by the Party and the government; we are deprived of only one right, the right to write badly. "Comrades," he said, "let us not fool ourselves: this is a very important right, and to take it away from us is no small thing." And he said, "Let us give up this right, and may God help us. And if there is no God, let us help ourselves. . . ."

The right to write badly—how precious it seems when once there has been the need to conceive of it! Upon the right to write badly depends the right to write at all. There must have been many in the audience who understood how serious and how terrible Babel's joke was. And there must have been some who had felt a chill at their hearts at another joke that Babel had made earlier in his address, when he spoke of himself as practicing a new literary genre. This was the genre of silence—he was, he said, "the master of the genre of silence."

Thus he incriminated himself for his inability to work. He made reference to the doctrine that the writer must have respect for the reader, and he said that it was a correct doctrine. He himself, he said, had a very highly developed respect for the reader; so much so, indeed, that it might be said of him that he suffered from a hyper-trophy of the faculty of respect—"I have so much respect for the reader that I am dumb." But then he takes a step beyond irony; he ventures to interpret, and by his interpretation to challenge, the social doctrine of "respect for the reader." The reader, he says, asks for bread, and he should indeed be given what he asks for, but not in the way he expects it. He must be surprised by what he gets; he ought not be given what he can easily recognize as "a certified true copy" of life—the essence of art is unexpectedness.

The silence for which Babel apologized was not broken. In 1937 he was arrested. He died in a concentration camp in 1939 or 1940. It is not known for certain whether he was shot or died of typhus. Both accounts of the manner of his death have been given by people who were inmates of the camp at the time. Nor is it known for what specific reason he was arrested. Raymond Rosenthal, in an admirable essay on Babel published in *Commentary* in 1947, says, on good authority, that Babel did not undergo a purge but was arrested for having made a politically indiscreet remark. It has been said that he was arrested when Yagoda was purged, because he was having a love-affair with Yagoda's sister. It has also been said that he was accused of Trotskyism, which does indeed seem possible, especially if we think of Trotsky as not only a political but a cultural figure.[2]

But it may be that no reason for the last stage of the extinction of Isaac Babel need be looked for beyond that which is provided by his stories, by their method and style. If ever we want to remind ourselves of the nature and power of art, we have only to think of how accurate reactionary governments are in their awareness of that nature and that power. It is not merely the content of art that they fear, not merely explicit doctrine, but whatever of energy and autonomy is implied by the aesthetic qualities a work may have. Intensity, irony, and ambiguousness, for example, constitute a clear threat to the impassivity of the state. They constitute a *secret*.

Babel was not a political man except as every man of intelligence was political at the time of the Revolution. Except, too, as every man of talent or genius is political who makes his heart a battleground for conflicting tendencies of culture. In Babel's heart there was a kind of fighting—he was captivated by the vision of two ways of being, the way of violence and the way of peace, and he was torn between them. The conflict between the two ways of being was an essential element of his mode of thought. And when Soviet culture

---

[2] In the introduction to her edition in English of Babel's letters to his family, *The Lonely Years,* 1964, Miss Nathalia Babel, his daughter by his first marriage, says that it is not true that Babel had an affair with Yagoda's sister. Although Babel's life and work have in recent years been quite intensively studied by Western scholars of Soviet literature, I believe that the actual reasons for the arrest have not yet been disclosed.

was brought under full discipline, the fighting in Babel's heart could not be permitted to endure. It was a subversion of discipline. It implied that there was more than one way of being. It hinted that one might live in doubt, that one might live by means of a question.

It is with some surprise that we become aware of the centrality of the cultural, the moral, the *personal* issue in Babel's work, for what strikes us first is the intensity of his specifically aesthetic preoccupation. In his schooldays Babel was passionate in his study of French literature; for several years he wrote his youthful stories in French, his chief masters being Flaubert and Maupassant. When, in an autobiographical sketch, he means to tell us that he began his mature work in 1923, he puts it that in that year he began to express his thoughts "clearly, and not at great length." This delight in brevity became his peculiar mark. When Eisenstein spoke of what it was that literature might teach the cinema, he said that "Isaac Babel will speak of the extreme laconicism of literature's expressive means—Babel, who, perhaps, knows in practice better than anyone else that great secret, 'that there is no iron that can enter the human heart with such stupefying effect, as a period placed at just the right moment.' "[3] A reminiscence of Babel by Konstantin Paustovski tells of his intense admiration of Kipling's "iron prose" and of his sense of affinity with the style of Julius Caesar.[4] Babel's love of the laconic implies certain other elements of his aesthetic, his commitment (it is sometimes excessive) to *le mot juste,* to the search for the word or phrase that will do its work with a ruthless speed, and his remarkable powers of significant distortion, the rapid foreshortening, the striking displacement of interest and shift of emphasis—in general his pulling all awry the arrangement of things as they appear in the "certified true copy."

Babel's preoccupation with form, with the aesthetic surface, is, we soon see, entirely at the service of his moral concern. James Joyce has

[3] Eisenstein quotes from Babel's story, "Guy de Maupassant." The reference to Babel occurs in the essay of 1932, "A Course in Treatment," in the volume *Film Form: Essays in Film Theory,* edited and translated by Jay Leyda, 1949.

[4] This was kindly communicated to me in translation by Mrs. Rachel Erlich.

taught us the word *epiphany,* a showing forth—Joyce had the "theory" that suddenly, almost miraculously, by a phrase or a gesture, a life might thrust itself through the veil of things and for an instant show itself forth, startling us by its existence. In itself the conception of the epiphany makes a large statement about the nature of human life; it suggests that the human fact does not dominate the scene of our existence—for something to "show forth" it must first be hidden, and the human fact is submerged in and subordinated to a world of circumstance, the world of *things;* it is known only in glimpses, emerging from the danger or the sordidness in which it is implicated. Those writers who by their practice subscribe to the theory of the epiphany are drawn to a particular aesthetic. In the stories of Maupassant, as in those of Stephen Crane, and Hemingway, and the Joyce of *Dubliners,* as in those of Babel himself, we perceive the writer's intention to create a form which shall in itself be shapely and autonomous and at the same time unusually responsible to the truth of external reality, the truth of things and events. To this end he concerns himself with the given moment, and, seeming almost hostile to the continuity of time, he presents the past only as it can be figured in the present. In his commitment to event he affects to be indifferent to "meanings" and "values"; he seems to be saying that although he can tell us with unusual accuracy what is going on, he does not presume to interpret it, scarcely to understand it, certainly not to judge it. He arranges that the story shall tell itself, as it were; or he tells it by means of a narrator who somehow makes it clear that he has no personal concern with the outcome of events—what I have called Babel's lyric joy in the midst of violence is in effect one of his devices for achieving the tone of detachment. We are not, of course, for very long deceived by the elaborate apparatus contrived to suggest the almost affectless detachment of the writer. We soon enough see what he is up to. His intense concern with the hard aesthetic surface of the story, his preoccupation with things and events, are, we begin to perceive, cognate with the universe, representative of its nature, of the unyielding circumstance in which the human fact exists; they make the condition for the epiphany, the showing forth; and the apparent denial of immediate pathos is a condition of the ultimate pathos the writer conceives.

All this, as I say, is soon enough apparent in Babel's stories. And yet, even when we have become aware of his pathos, we are, I think, surprised by the kind of moral issue that lies beneath the brilliant surface of the stories, beneath the lyric and ironic elegance—we are surprised by its elemental simplicity. We are surprised, too, by its passionate subjectivity, the intensity of the author's personal involvement, his defenseless commitment of himself to the issue.

The stories of *Red Cavalry* have as their principle of coherence what I have called the anomaly, or the joke, of a Jew who is a member of a Cossack regiment—Babel was a supply officer under General Budenny in the campaign of 1920. Traditionally the Cossack was the feared and hated enemy of the Jew. But he was more than that. The principle of his existence stood in total antithesis to the principle of the Jew's existence. The Jew conceived his own ideal character to consist in his being intellectual, pacific, humane. The Cossack was physical, violent, without mind or manners. When a Jew of Eastern Europe wanted to say what we mean by "a bull in a china shop," he said "a Cossack in a *succah*"—in, that is, one of the fragile decorated booths or tabernacles in which the meals of the harvest festival of Succoth are eaten: he intended an image of animal violence, of aimless destructiveness. And if the Jew was political, if he thought beyond his own ethnic and religious group, he knew that the Cossack was the enemy not only of the Jew—although him especially—but of all men who thought of freedom; he was the natural and appropriate instrument of ruthless oppression.

There was, of course, another possible view of the Cossack, one that had its appeal for many Russian intellectuals, although it was not likely to win the assent of the Jew. Tolstoi had represented the Cossack as having a primitive energy, passion, and virtue. He was the man as yet untrammeled by civilization, direct, immediate, fierce. He was the man of enviable simplicity, the man of the body—and of the horse, the man who moved with speed and grace. We have devised an image of our lost freedom which we mock in the very phrase by which we name it: the noble savage. No doubt the mockery is justified, yet our fantasy of the noble savage represents a reality of our existence, it stands for our sense of something un-happily surrendered, the truth of the body, the truth of full sexual-ity, the truth of open aggressiveness. Babel's view of the Cossack was more consonant with that of Tolstoi than with the traditional view of his own people. For him the Cossack was indeed the noble savage, all too savage, not often noble, yet having in his savagery some quality that might raise strange questions in a Jewish mind.

I have seen three pictures of Babel, and it is a puzzle to know how he was supposed to look. The most convincing of the pictures is a photograph, to which the two official portrait-sketches bear but little resemblance. The sketch which serves as the frontispiece to Babel's volume of stories of 1932 makes the author look like a Chinese merchant—his face is round, impassive, and priggish; his nose is low and flat; he stares through rimless glasses with immovable gaze. The sketch in the *Soviet Literary Encyclopedia* lengthens his face and gives him horn-rimmed spectacles and an air of amused and knowing assurance: a well-educated and successful Hollywood writer who has made the intelligent decision not to apologize for his profession except by his smile. But in the photograph the face is very long and thin, charged with emotion and internality; bitter, intense, very sensitive, touched with humor, full of consciousness and con-tradiction. It is "typically" an intellectual's face, a scholar's face, and it has great charm. I should not want to speak of it as a Jewish face, but it is a kind of face which many Jews used to aspire to have, or hoped their sons would have. It was, surely, this face, or one much like it, that Babel took with him when he went among the Cossacks.[5]

---

[5] Apparently it was hard to know what Babel looked like even if one met him face to face. Here is Paustovski trying to cope with the difficulty: "I had never met a person who looked less like a writer than Babel. Stocky, almost no neck . . . a wrinkled forehead, an oily twinkle in the small eyes; he did not arouse any in-terest. He could be taken for a salesman, a broker. But of course this was true only

We can only marvel over the vagary of the military mind by which Isaac Babel came to be assigned as a supply officer to a Cossack regiment. He was a Jew of the ghetto. As a boy—so he tells us in his autobiographical stories—he had been of stunted growth, physically inept, subject to nervous disorders. He was an intellectual, a writer—a man, as he puts it in striking phrase, with spectacles on his nose and autumn in his heart. The orders that sent him to General Budenny's command were drawn either by a conscious and ironical Destiny with a literary bent—or at his own personal request. For the reasons that made it bizarre that he should have been attached to a Cossack regiment are the reasons why he was there. He was there to be submitted to a test, he was there to be initiated. He was there because of the dreams of his boyhood. Babel's talent, like that of many modern writers, is rooted in the memory of boyhood, and Babel's boyhood was more than usually dominated by the idea of the test and the initiation. We might put it that Babel rode with a Cossack regiment because, when he was nine years old, he had seen his father kneeling before a Cossack captain who wore lemon-colored chamois gloves and looked ahead with the gaze of one who rides through a mountain pass.[6]

Isaac Babel was born in Odessa, in 1894. The years following the accession of Nicholas II were dark years indeed for the Jews of Russia. It was the time of the bitterest official anti-Semitism, of the Pale, of the Beilis trial, of the Black Hundreds and the planned pogroms. And yet in Odessa the Jewish community may be said to have flourished. Odessa was the great port of the Black Sea, an eastern Marseilles or Naples, and in such cities the transient, heterogeneous population dilutes the force of law and tradition, for good

---

as long as he didn't open his mouth. . . . Many people could not look into Babel's burning eyes. He was by nature an 'unmasker,' he liked to put people into impossible positions and he had the reputation of being a difficult and dangerous person. . . . Then Babel took off his glasses, and his face became at once helpless and good. . . ."

[6] Miss Nathalia Babel denies that Babel was being literally autobiographical in the stories in which he speaks in the first person of the experiences of a boy-protagonist; she casts particular doubt upon the narratives having to do with a pogrom.

as well as for bad. The Jews of Odessa were in some degree free to take part in the general life of the city. They were, to be sure, debarred from the schools, with but few exceptions. And they were sufficiently isolate when the passions of a pogrom swept the city. Yet all classes of the Jewish community seem to have been marked by a singular robustness and vitality, by a sense of the world, and of themselves in the world. The upper classes lived in affluence, sometimes in luxury, and it was possible for them to make their way into a Gentile society in which prejudice had been attenuated by cosmopolitanism. The intellectual life was of a particular energy, producing writers, scholars, and journalists of very notable gifts; it is in Odessa that modern Hebrew poetry takes its rise with Bialyk and Tchernichovski. As for the lower classes, Babel himself represents them as living freely and heartily. In their ghetto, the Moldavanka, they were far more conditioned by their economic circumstances than by their religious ties; they were not at all like the poor Jews of the *shtetln,* the little towns of Poland, whom Babel was later to see. These Odessa ghetto Jews are of a Brueghel-like bulk and brawn; they have large, coarse, elaborate nicknames; they are draymen and dairy-farmers; they are gangsters—the Jewish gangs of the Moldavanka were famous; they made upon the young Babel an ineradicable impression and to them he devoted a remarkable group of comic stories.

It was not Odessa, then, it was not even Odessa's ghetto, that forced upon Babel the image of the Jew as a man not in the actual world, a man of no body, a man of intellect, or wits, passive before his secular fate. Not even his image of the Jewish intellectual was substantiated by the Odessa actuality—Bialyk and Tchernichovski were anything but men with spectacles on their noses and autumn in their hearts, and no one who ever encountered in America the striking figure of Dr. Chaim Tchernowitz, the great scholar of the Talmud and formerly the Chief Rabbi of Odessa, a man of Jovian port and large, free mind, would be inclined to conclude that there was but a single season of the heart available to a Jew of Odessa.

But Babel had seen his father on his knees before a Cossack captain on a horse, who said, "At your service," and touched his fur cap with his yellow-gloved hand and politely paid no heed to the mob looting the Babel store. Such an experience, or even a far milder analogue of it, is determinative in the life of a boy. Freud speaks of the effect upon him when, at twelve, his father told of having accepted in a pacific way the insult of having his new fur cap knocked into the mud by a Gentile who shouted at him, "Jew, get off the pavement." It is clear that Babel's relation with his father defined his relation to his Jewishness. Benya Krik, the greatest of the gangsters, he who was called King, was a Jew of Odessa, but he did not wear glasses and he did not have autumn in his heart—it is in writing about Benya that Babel uses the phrase that sets so far apart the intellectual and the man of action. The exploration of Benya's pre-eminence among gangsters does indeed take account of his personal endowment—Benya was a "lion," a "tiger," a "cat"; he "could spend the night with a Russian woman and satisfy her." But what really made his fate was his having had Mendel Krik, the drayman, for his faher. "What does such a father think about? He thinks about drinking a good glass of vodka, of smashing somebody in the face, of his horses—and nothing more. You want to live and he makes you die twenty times a day. What would you have done in Benya Krik's place? You would have done nothing. But *he* did something. . . ." But Babel's father did not think about vodka, and smashing somebody in the face, and horses; he thought about large and serious things, among them respectability and fame. He was a shopkeeper, not well to do, a serious man, a failure. The sons of such men have much to prove, much to test themselves for, and, if they are Jewish, their Jewishness is ineluctably involved in the test.

Babel spoke with bitterness of the terrible discipline of his Jewish education. He thought of the Talmud Torah as a prison shutting him off from all desirable life, from reality itself. One of the stories he tells—perhaps the incident was invented to stand for his feelings about his Jewish schooling—is about his father's having fallen prey to the Messianic delusion which beset the Jewish families of Odessa, the belief that any one of them might produce a prodigy of the violin, a little genius who could be sent to be processed by Professor Auer in Petersburg, who would play before crowned heads in a velvet suit, and support his family in honor and comfort. Such miracles occurred in Odessa, whence came Elman, Zimbalist, and Heifetz. Babel's father hoped for wealth, but he would have forgone wealth if he could have been sure, at a minimum, of fame. Being small, the young Babel at fourteen might pass for eight and a prodigy. In point of fact, Babel had not even talent, and certainly no vocation. He was repelled by the idea of becoming a musical "dwarf," one of the "big-headed freckled children with necks as thin as flower stalks and an epileptic flush on their cheeks." This was a Jewish fate and he fled from it, escaping to the port and the beaches of Odessa. Here he tried to learn to swim and could not: "the hydrophobia of my ancestors—Spanish rabbis and Frankfurt moneychangers—dragged me to the bottom." But a kindly proof-reader, an elderly man who loved nature and children, took pity on him. "How d'you mean, the water won't hold you? Why shouldn't it hold you?"—his specific gravity was no different from anybody else's and the good Yefim Nikitich Smolich taught him to swim. "I came to love that man," Babel says in one of the very few of his sentences over which no slightest irony plays, "with the love that only a boy suffering from hysteria and headaches can feel for a real man."

The story is called "Awakening" and it commemorates the boy's first effort of creation. It is to Nikitich that he shows the tragedy he has composed and it is the old man who observes that the boy has talent but no knowledge of nature and who undertakes to teach him how to tell one tree or one plant from another. This ignorance of the natural world—Babel refers to it again in his autobiographical sketch—was a Jewish handicap to be overcome. It was not an ex-travagance of Jewish self-consciousness that led him to make the generalization—Maurice Samuel remarks in *The World of Sholom*

Aleichem that in the Yiddish vocabulary of the Jews of eastern Europe there are but two flower names (rose, violet) and no names for wild birds.

When it was possible to do so, Babel left his family and Odessa to live the precarious life, especially precarious for a Jew, of a Russian artist and intellectual. He went to Kiev and then, in 1915, he ventured to St. Petersburg without a residence certificate. He was twenty-one. He lived in a cellar on Pushkin Street, and wrote stories which were everywhere refused until Gorki took him up and in 1916 published two stories in his magazine. To Gorki, Babel said, he was indebted for everything. But Gorki became of the opinion that Babel's first work was successful only by accident; he advised the young man to abandon the career of literature and to "go among the people." Babel served in the Czar's army on the Rumanian front; after the Revolution he was for a time a member of the Cheka; he went on grain-collecting expeditions in 1918; he fought with the northern army against Yudenich. In 1920 he was with Budenny in Poland, twenty-six years old, having seen much, having endured much, yet demanding initiation, submitting himself to the test.

The test, it is important to note, is not that of courage. Babel's affinity with Stephen Crane and Hemingway is close in many respects, of which not the least important is his feeling for his boyhood and for the drama of the boy's initiation into manhood. But the question that Babel puts to himself is not the one that means so much to the two American writers; he does not ask whether he will be able to meet danger with honor. This he seems to know he can do. Rather, the test is of his power of direct and immediate, and violent, action—not whether he can endure being killed but whether he can endure killing. In the story "After the Battle" a Cossack comrade is enraged against him not because, in the recent engagement, he had hung back, but because he had ridden with an unloaded revolver. The story ends with the narrator imploring fate to "grant me the simplest of proficiencies—the ability to kill my fellow men."

The necessity for submitting to the test is very deeply rooted in Babel's psychic life. This becomes readily apparent when we read the whole of Babel's canon and perceive the manifest connection between certain of the incidents of *Red Cavalry* and those of the stories of the Odessa boyhood. In the story "My First Goose" the newcomer to the brigade is snubbed by the brilliant Cossack commander because he is a man with spectacles on his nose, an intellectual. "Not a life for the brainy type here," says the quartermaster who carries his trunk to his billet. "But you go and mess up a lady, and a good lady too, and you'll have the boys patting you on the back. . . ." The five new comrades in the billet make it quite clear that he is an outsider and unwanted, they begin at once to bully and haze him. Yet by one action he overcomes their hostility to him and his spectacles. He asks the old landlady for food and she puts him off; whereupon he kills the woman's goose in a particularly brutal manner, and, picking it up on the point of a sword, thrusts it at the woman and orders her to cook it. Now the crisis is passed; the price of community has been paid. The group of five re-forms itself to become a group of six. All is decent and composed in the conduct of the men. There is a general political discussion, then sleep. "We slept, all six of us, beneath a wooden roof that let in the stars, warming one another, our legs intermingled. I dreamed: and in my dreams I saw women. But my heart, stained with bloodshed, grated and brimmed over." We inevitably read this story in the light of Babel's two connected stories of the 1905 pogrom, "The Story of My Dovecot" and "First Love," recalling the scene in which the crippled cigarette vender, whom all the children loved, crushes the boy's newly bought and long-desired pigeon and flings it in his face. Later the pigeon's blood and entrails are washed from the boy's cheek by the young Russian woman who is sheltering the Babel family and whom the boy adores. It is after her caress that the boy sees his father on his knees before the Cossack captain; the story ends with his capitulation to nervous illness. And now again a bird has been brutally killed, now again the killing is linked with sexuality, but now it is not his bird but another's, now he is not passive but active.

Yet no amount of understanding of the psychological genesis of the act of killing the goose makes it easy for us to judge it as anything more than a very ugly brutality. It is not easy for us—and it is not easy for Babel. Not easy, but we must make the effort to comprehend that for Babel it is not violence in itself that is at issue in his relation to the Cossacks, but something else, some quality with which violence does indeed go along, but which is not in itself merely violent. This quality, whatever it is to be called, is of the greatest importance in Babel's conception of himself as an intellectual and an artist, in his conception of himself as a Jew.

It is, after all, not merely violence and brutality that make the Cossacks what they are. This is not the first violence and brutality that Babel has known—when it comes to violence and brutality a Western reader can scarcely have, unless he sets himself to acquire it, an adequate idea of their place in the life of eastern Europe. The impulse to violence, as we have learned, seems indigenous in all mankind. Among certain groups the impulse is far more freely licensed than among others. Americans are aware and ashamed of the actuality or potentiality of violence in their own culture, but it is as nothing to that of the East of Europe; the people for whom the mass impalings and the knout are part of their memory of the exercise of authority over them have their own ways of expressing their rage. As compared with what the knife, or the homemade pike, or the boot, can do, the revolver is an instrument of delicate amenity and tender mercy—this, indeed, is the point of one of Babel's stories. Godfrey Blunden's description of the method of execution used by the Ukrainian peasant bands is scarcely to be read.

The point I would make is that the Cossacks were not exceptional for their violence. It was not their violence in itself that evoked Tolstoi's admiration. Nor was it what fascinated Babel. Rather he was drawn by what the violence goes along with, the boldness, the passionateness, the simplicity and directness—and the grace. Thus the story "My First Goose" opens with a description of the masculine charm of the brigade commander Savitsky. His male grace is celebrated in a shower of tropes—the "beauty of his giant's body" is fully particularized: we hear of the decorated chest "cleaving the hut as a standard cleaves the sky," of "the iron and flower of that youthfulness," of the long legs, which were "like girls sheathed to the neck in shining riding boots." Only the openness of the admiration and envy—which constitutes, also, a qualifying irony—keeps the description from seeming sexually perverse. It is remarkably *not* perverse; it is as "healthy" as a boy's love of his hero of the moment. And Savitsky's grace is a real thing. Babel has no wish to destroy it by any of the means which are so ready to the intellectual confronted by this kind of power and charm; he does not diminish the glory he perceives by confronting it with the pathos of human creatures less glorious physically, having more, or a higher, moral appeal because they are weaker and because they suffer.

The grace that Babel saw and envied in the Cossacks is much the same thing that D. H. Lawrence was drawn to in his imagination of archaic cultures and personalities and of the ruthlessness, even the cruelty, that attended their grace. It is what Yeats had in mind in his love of "the old disturbed exalted life, the old splendor." It is what even the gentle Forster represents in the brilliant scene in *Where Angels Fear to Tread* in which Gino, the embodiment of male grace, tortures Stephen by twisting his broken arm.

Babel carries as far as he can his sympathy with the fantasy that an ultimate psychic freedom is to be won through cruelty conceived of as a spiritual exercise. One of the famous and fascinating leaders of horse is "the headstrong Pavlichenko" who tells of his peasant origin, of the insults received from his aristocratic landlord, of how, when the Revolution came, he had wiped out the insult. "Then I stamped on my master Nikitinsky; trampled on him for an hour or maybe more. And in that time I got to know life through and through. With shooting . . . you only get rid of a chap. Shooting's letting him off, and too damn easy for yourself. With shooting you'll never get at the soul, to where it is in a fellow and how it shows itself. But I don't spare myself, and I've more than once trampled an enemy for over an hour. You see, I want to get to know what life really is. . . ." This is all too *raffiné*—we are inclined, I think, to forget Pavlichenko and to be a little revolted by Babel.[7]

In our effort to understand Babel's complex involvement with the Cossack ethos we must be aware of the powerful and obsessive significance that violence has for the intellectual. Violence, is, of course, the contradiction of the intellectual's characteristic enterprise of rationality. Yet at the same time it is the very image of that enterprise. This may seem a strange thing to say. Since Plato we have set violence and reason over against each other in reciprocal negation. Yet it is Plato who can tell us why there is affinity between them. In the most famous of the Platonic myths, the men of the Cave are seated facing the interior wall of the Cave, and they are chained by their necks so that it is impossible for them to turn their heads. They can face in but one direction, they can see nothing but the shadows that are cast on the wall by the fire behind them. A man comes to them who has somehow freed himself and gone into the world outside the Cave. He brings them news of the light of the sun; he tells them that there are things to be seen which are real, that what they see on the wall are but shadows. Plato says that the men chained in the Cave will not believe this news. They insist that it is not possible, that the shadows are the only reality. But suppose they do believe the news! Then how violent they will become against their chains as they struggle to free themselves so that they may look at what they believe is there to be seen. They will think of violence as part of their bitter effort to know what is real. To grasp, to seize—to *apprehend,* as we say—reality from out of the deep dark cave of the mind—this is indeed a very violent action.

---

[7] The celebration of the Cossack ethos gave no satisfaction to General Budenny, who, when some of Babel's *Red Cavalry* stories appeared in a magazine before their publication in a volume, attacked Babel furiously, and with a large display of literary pretentiousness, for the cultural corruption and political ignorance which, he claimed, the stories displayed.

The artist in our time is perhaps more overtly concerned with the apprehension of reality than the philosopher is, and the image of violence seems often an appropriate way of representing his mode of perception. "The language of poetry naturally falls in with the language of power," says Hazlitt in his lecture on *Coriolanus* and goes on to speak in several brilliant passages of "the logic of the imagination and the passions" which makes them partisan with representations of proud strength. Hazlitt carries his generalization beyond the warrant of literary fact yet all that he says is pertinent to Babel, who almost always speaks of art in the language of force. The unexpectedness which he takes to be the essence of art is that of a surprise attack. He speaks of the maneuvers of prose, of "the army of words, . . . the army in which all kinds of weapons may be brought into play." In one of his most remarkable stories, "Di Grasso," he describes the performance of a banal play given by an Italian troupe in Odessa; all is dreariness until in the third act the hero sees his betrothed in converse with the villainous seducer, and, leaping miraculously, with the power of levitation of a Nijinsky or a panther, soars across the stage and drops upon the villain to destroy him. That leap of the actor Di Grasso makes the fortune of the Italian company with the exigent Odessa audience; that leap, we are given to understand, is art. And as the story continues, Babel is explicit—if also ironic—in what he demonstrates of the moral effect that may be produced by this violence of virtuosity and power.

The spectacles on his nose were for Babel of the first importance in his conception of himself. He was a man to whom the perception of the world outside the Cave came late and had to be apprehended, by strength and speed, against the parental or cultural interdiction, the Jewish interdiction. The violence of the Revolution, its sudden leap, was cognate with this feral passion for perception—to an artist the Revolution might well have seemed the rending not only of the social but of the perceptual chains, those that held men's gaze upon the shadows on the wall; it may have suggested the rush of men from the darkness of the Cave into the light of reality. Something of this is conveyed in a finely wrought story, "Line and Color," in which Kerenski is represented as defending his myopia, refusing to wear glasses, because, as he argues very charmingly, there is so much that myopia protects him from seeing; imagination and benign illusion are thus given a larger license. But at a great meeting in the first days of the Revolution he cannot perceive the disposition of the crowd and the story ends with Trotsky coming to the rostrum and saying in his implacable voice, "Comrades!"

But when we have followed Babel into the depths of his experience of violence, when we have imagined something of what it meant in his psychic life and in the developing conception of his art, we must be no less aware of his experience of the principle that stands opposed to the Cossack principle.

We can scarcely fail to see that when in the stories of *Red Cavalry* Babel submits the ethos of the intellectual to the criticism of the Cossack ethos, he intends a criticism of his own ethos not merely as an intellectual but as a Jew. It is always as an intellectual, never as a Jew, that he is denounced by his Cossack comrades, but we know that he has either suppressed, for political reasons, the denunciations of him as a Jew that were actually made, or, if none were actually made, that he has in his heart supposed that they were made. These criticisms of the Jewish ethos, as he embodies it, Babel believes to have no small weight. When he implores fate to grant him the simplest of proficiencies, the ability to kill his fellow man, we are likely to take this as nothing but an irony, and as an ironic assertion of the superiority of his moral instincts. But it is only in part an irony. There comes a moment when he should kill a fellow man. In "The Death of Dolgushov," a comrade lies propped against a tree; he cannot be moved, inevitably he must die, for his entrails are hanging out; he must be left behind and he asks for a bullet in his head so that the Poles will not "play their dirty tricks" on him. It is the narrator whom he asks for the *coup de grâce,* but the narrator flees and sends a friend, who, when he has done what had to be done, turns on the "sensitive" man in a fury of rage and disgust.

"You bastards in spectacles have about as much pity for us as a cat has for a mouse." Or again, the narrator has incurred the enmity of a comrade through no actual fault—no moral fault—of his own, merely through having been assigned a mount that the other man passionately loved, and riding it so badly that it developed saddle galls. Now the horse has been returned, but the man does not forgive him, and the narrator asks a superior officer to compound the quarrel. He is rebuffed. "You're trying to live without enemies," he is told. "That's all you think about, not having enemies." It comes at us with momentous force. This time we are not misled into supposing that Babel intends irony and a covert praise of his pacific soul; we know that in this epiphany of his refusal to accept enmity he means to speak adversely of himself in his Jewish character.

But his Jewish character is not the same as the Jewish character of the Jews of Poland. To these Jews he comes with all the presuppositions of an acculturated Jew of Odessa, which were perhaps not much different from the suppositions of an acculturated Jew of Germany. He is repelled by the conditions of their life; he sees them as physically uncouth and warped; many of them seem to him to move "monkey-fashion." Sometimes he affects a wondering alienation from them, as when he speaks of "the occult crockery that the Jews use only once a year at Eastertime." His complexity and irony being what they are, the Jews of Poland are made to justify the rejection of the Jews among whom he was reared and the wealthy assimilated Jews of Petersburg. "The image of the stout and jovial Jews of the South, bubbling like cheap wine, takes shape in my memory, in sharp contrast to the bitter scorn inherent in these long bony backs, these tragic yellow beards." Yet the Jews of Poland are more than a stick with which Babel beats his own Jewish past. They come to exist for him as a spiritual fact of consummate value.

Almost in the degree that Babel is concerned with violence in the stories of *Red Cavalry,* he is concerned with spirituality. It is not only Jewish spirituality that draws him. A considerable number of the stories have to do with churches, and although they do indeed often express the anticlerical feeling expectable in the revolutionary circumstances, the play of Babel's irony permits him to respond in a positive way to the aura of religion. "The breath of an invisible order of things," he says in one story, "glimmers beneath the crumbling ruin of the priest's house, and its soothing seduction unmanned me." He is captivated by the ecclesiastical painter Pan Apolek, he who created ecclesiastical scandals by using the publicans and sinners of the little towns as the models for his saints and Virgins. Yet it is chiefly the Jews who speak to him of the life beyond violence, and even Pan Apolek's "heretical and intoxicating brush" had achieved its masterpiece in his Christ of the Berestechko church, "the most extraordinary image of God I had ever seen in my life," a curly-headed Jew, a bearded figure in a Polish greatcoat of orange, barefoot, with torn and bleeding mouth, running from an angry mob with a hand raised to ward off a blow.

Hazlitt, in the passage to which I have referred, speaking of the "logic of the imagination and the passions," says that we are naturally drawn to the representation of what is strong and proud and feral. Actually that is not so: we are, rather, drawn to the representation of what is real. It was a new species of reality that Babel found in the Jews of the Polish provinces. "In these passionate, anguish-chiseled features there is no fat, no warm pulsing of blood. The Jews of Volhynia and Galicia move jerkily, in an uncontrolled and uncouth way; but their capacity for suffering is full of a somber greatness, and their unvoiced contempt for the Polish gentry unbounded."

Here is the counter-image to the captivating Savitsky, the denial of the pride in the glory of the flesh to which, early or late, every artist comes, to which he cannot come in full sincerity unless he can also make full affirmation of the glory. Here too is the image of art that is counter to that of Di Grasso's leap, counter to the language armed to stab—it is through the Jews of the Polish provinces that Babel tells us of the artist's suffering, patience, uncouthness, and scorn.

If Babel's experience with the Cossacks may be understood as having reference to the boy's relation to his father, his experience of the Jews of Poland has, we cannot but feel, a maternal reference. To the one, Babel responds as a boy; to the other, as a child. In the story "Gedali" he speaks with open sentimentality of his melancholy on the eve of Sabbaths—"On those evenings my child's heart was rocked like a little ship upon enchanted waves. O the rotted Talmuds of my childhood! O the dense melancholy of memories." And when he has found a Jew, it is one who speaks to him in this fashion: ". . . All is mortal. Only the mother is destined to immortality. And when the mother is no longer living, she leaves a memory which none yet has dared to sully. The memory of the mother nourishes in us a compassion that is like the ocean, and the measureless ocean feeds the rivers that dissect the universe."

He has sought the Jew Gedali in his gutted curiosity shop ("Where was your kindly shade that evening, Dickens?") to ask for "a Jewish glass of tea, and a little of that pensioned-off God in a glass of tea." He does not, that evening, get what he asks for; what he does get is a discourse on revolution, on the impossibility of a revolution made in blood, on the International that is never to be realized, the International of the good.

It was no doubt the easier for Babel to respond to the spiritual life of the Jews of Poland because it was a life coming to its end and having about it the terrible pathos of its death. He makes no pretense that it could ever claim him for its own. But it established itself in his heart as an image, beside the image of the other life that also could not claim him, the Cossack life. The opposition of these two images made his art—but it was not a dialectic that his Russia could permit.

The Leavis-Snow
Controversy

I

IT IS now nearly eighty years since Matthew Arnold came to America on his famous lecture tour. Of his repertory of three lectures, none was calculated to give unqualified pleasure to his audience. The lecture on Emerson praised the then most eminent of American writers only after it had denied that he was a literary figure of the first order. The lecture called "Numbers" raised disturbing questions about the relation of democracy to excellence and distinction. "Literature and Science" was the least likely to give offense, yet even this most memorable of the three *Discourses in America* was not without its touch of uncomfortableness. In 1883 America was by no means committed—and, indeed, never was to be committed—to the belief that the right education for the modern age must be predominantly scientific and technical, and Arnold, when he cited the proponents of this idea, which of course he opposed, mentioned only those who were English. Yet his audience surely knew that Arnold was warning them against what would seem to be the natural tendency of an industrial democracy to devalue the old "aristocratic" education in favor of studies that are merely practical.

Arnold wrote "Emerson" and "Numbers" especially for his American tour, but he had first composed "Literature and Science" as the

Rede Lecture at Cambridge in 1882. Its original occasion cannot fail to have a peculiar interest at this moment, for C. P. Snow's *The Two Cultures and the Scientific Revolution,* around which so curious a storm rages in England, was the Rede Lecture of 1959.

Sir Charles did not mention his great predecessor in the lectureship, although his own discourse was exactly on Arnold's subject and took a line exactly the opposite of Arnold's. And F. R. Leavis, whose admiration of Arnold is well known and whose position in respect to the relative importance of literature and of science in education is much the same as Arnold's, did not mention Arnold either, when, in his Richmond Lecture at Downing College, he launched an attack of unexampled ferocity upon the doctrine and the author of *The Two Cultures.*

In its essential terms, the issue in debate has not changed since Arnold spoke. Arnold's chief antagonist was T. H. Huxley—it was he who, in his lecture "Culture and Education," had said that literature should, and inevitably would, step down from its preeminent place in education, that science and not "culture" must supply the knowledge which is necessary for an age committed to rational truth and material practicality. What is more, Huxley said, science will supply the very basis of the assumptions of modern ethics. In effect Snow says nothing different.

The word "culture" had been Arnold's personal insigne ever since the publication of *Culture and Anarchy* in 1867, and Huxley made particular reference to the views on the value of humanistic study which Arnold had expressed in that book.[1] Arnold's reply in "Literature and Science" could not have been simpler, just as it could not have been more temperate, although it surely did not surpass in temperateness Huxley's statement of his disagreement with Arnold's ideas; the two men held each other in high admira-

[1] Arnold, I need scarcely say, did not use the word in the modern sense in which it is used by anthropologists, sociologists, and historians of thought and art; this is, more or less, the sense in which it is used by Snow. For Arnold, "culture" was "the best that has been thought and said in the world" and also an individual person's relation to this body of thought and expression. My own use of the word in this essay is not Arnold's.

tion and were warm friends. Arnold said that he had not the least disposition to propose that science be slighted in education. Quite apart from its practical value, scientific knowledge is naturally a delight to the mind, no doubt engaging certain mental temperaments more than others but holding out the promise of intellectual pleasure to all. Yet of itself science does not, as Arnold put it, "serve" the instinct for conduct and the instinct for beauty, or at least it does not serve these instincts as they exist in most men. This service, which includes the relating of scientific knowledge to the whole life of man, is rendered by culture, which is not to be thought of as confined to literature—to *belles lettres*—but as comprising all the humane intellectual disciplines. When Dr. Leavis asserts the primacy of the humanities in education, he refers more exclusively to literature than Arnold did, but in general effect his position is the same.

It may seem strange, and a little tiresome, that the debate of eighty years ago should be instituted again today. Yet it is perhaps understandable in view of the "scientific revolution" about which Sir Charles tells us. This revolution would seem to be one of the instances in which a change of quantity becomes a change in kind— science can now do so much more and do it so much more quickly than it could a generation ago, let alone in the last century, that it has been transmuted from what the world has hitherto known. One of the consequences of this change—to Sir Charles it is the most salient of all possible consequences—is the new social hope that is now held out to us, of life made better in material respects, not merely in certain highly developed countries but all over the world and among peoples that at the moment are, by Western standards, scarcely developed at all.

The new power of science perhaps justifies a contemporary revival of the Victorian question. But if we consent to involve ourselves in the new dialectic of the old controversy, we must be aware that we are not addressing ourselves to a question of educational theory, or to an abstract contention as to what kind of knowledge has the truest affinity with the human soul. We approach these matters only to pass through them. What we address ourselves to is politics, and politics of a quite ultimate kind, and to the disposition of the modern mind.

II

The Two Cultures has had a very considerable currency in England and America ever since its publication in 1959, and in England it was for a time the subject of lively discussion. Indeed, the general agreement in England that it was a statement of great importance, to the point of its being used as an assigned text in secondary schools, was what aroused Dr. Leavis to make his assault on the lecture this long after the first interest in it had subsided. The early discussions of *The Two Cultures* were of a substantive kind, but the concerns which now agitate the English in response to Dr. Leavis's attack have scarcely anything to do with literature and science, or with education, or with social hope. These matters have now been made a mere subordinate element in what amounts to a scandal over a breach of manners. The published comments on Dr. Leavis's attack on *The Two Cultures* were, with few exceptions, directed to such considerations as the exact degree of monstrousness which Dr. Leavis achieved in speaking of Sir Charles as he did; whether or not he spoke out of envy of Sir Charles's reputation; whether or not he has, or deserves to have, any real standing as a critic; or writes acceptable English; or represents, as he claims he does, "the essential Cambridge."

Dr. Leavis's Richmond Lecture, "The Significance of C. P. Snow," was delivered in the Hall of Downing College, Cambridge, on February 28, 1962, and published in *The Spectator* of March 9.[2] In the next week's issue of *The Spectator,* seventeen letters appeared,

---

[2] In an editorial note, Dr. Leavis is quoted as saying, "The lecture was private and representatives of the press who inquired were informed that there was no admission and that no reporting was to be permitted. The appearance in newspapers of garbled reports has made it desirable that the lecture should appear in full."

all defending Snow and most of them expressing anger at, or contempt for, Leavis. The following week brought fifteen more communications, of which eight expressed partisanship with Leavis; several of these deplored the tone of the previous week's correspondence. Many of the correspondents who defended Snow were of distinguished reputation; of the defenders of Leavis, the only one known to me was Mr. Geoffrey Wagner, who wrote from America to communicate his belief that the attack on Snow was much needed, for, despite a parody in *New Left Review* in which Snow appears as C. P. Sleet, despite, too, his own adverse criticism of Snow in *The Critic,* "the hosannas obediently continued on this side of the Atlantic, both from the Barzun-Trilling syndrome and the Book-of-the-Month Club, the worst of both worlds, as it were." Three of the writers of the Snow party touched upon the question of literature and science, the scientist J. D. Bernal, the historian of science Stephen Toulmin, and the literary critic G. S. Fraser. In a miasma of personality-mongering, their letters afforded a degree of relief, but they said little that was of consequence. Of the Leavis party two dons of the University of Birmingham in a joint letter touched rapidly but with some cogency on the relation between literature and science, deploring any attempt to prefer one above the other, concluding that if one must be preferred, it should be, for reasons not stated, literature.

From the *Spectator* letters, so many of them expressing small and rather untidy passions, there are no doubt conclusions to be drawn, of a sufficiently depressing sort, about the condition of intellectual life at the moment. But no awareness that we may have of the generally bad state of intellectual affairs ought to blind us to the particular fault of Dr. Leavis in his treatment of Sir Charles Snow. Intelligent and serious himself, Dr. Leavis has in this instance been the cause of stupidity and triviality in other men.

There can be no two opinions about the tone in which Dr. Leavis deals with Sir Charles. It is a bad tone, an impermissible tone. It is bad in a personal sense because it is cruel—it manifestly intends to wound. It is bad intellectually because by its use Dr. Leavis has diverted attention, his own included, from the matter he sought to illuminate. The doctrine of *The Two Cultures* is a momentous one, and Dr. Leavis obscures its large significance by bringing into consideration such matters as Sir Charles's abilities as a novelist, his club membership, his opinion of his own talents, his worldly success, and his relation to worldly power. Anger, scorn, and an excessive consciousness of persons have always been elements of Dr. Leavis's thought—of the very process of his thought, not merely of his manner of expressing it. They were never exactly reassuring elements, but they could be set aside and made to seem of relatively small account in comparison with the remarkable cogency in criticism which Dr. Leavis so often achieved. But as they now appear in his valedictory address—for, in effect, that is what the Richmond Lecture was, since Dr. Leavis retired that year from his university post—they cannot be easily set aside, they stand in the way of what Dr. Leavis means to say.

And, indeed, our understanding of what he means to say is to be derived less from the passionate utterance of the lecture itself than from our knowledge of the whole direction of his career in criticism. That direction was from the first determined by Dr. Leavis's belief that the human faculty above all others to which literature addresses itself is the moral consciousness, which is also the source of all successful creation, the very root of poetic genius. The extent of his commitment to this idea results in what I believe to be a fault in his critical thought—he does not give anything like adequate recognition to those aspects of art which are gratuitous, which arise from high spirits and the impulse to play. One would suppose that the moral consciousness should, for its own purposes, take account of those aspects of art and life that do not fall within its dominion. But if the intensity of Dr. Leavis's commitment to the moral consciousness contrives to produce this deficiency of understanding, it is no less responsible for the accuracy and force which we recognize as the positive characteristics of his work. For Dr. Leavis, literature is what

Matthew Arnold said it is, *the criticism of life*—he can understand it in no other way. Both in all its simplicity and in all its hidden complexity, he has made Arnold's saying his own, and from it he has drawn his strength.

If, then, Dr. Leavis now speaks with a very special intensity in response to *The Two Cultures,* we must do him the justice of seeing that the Rede Lecture denies, and in an extreme way, all that he has ever believed about literature—it is, in fact, nothing less than an indictment of literature on social and moral grounds. It represents literature as constituting a danger to the national well-being, and most especially when it is overtly a criticism of life.

Not only because Charles Snow is himself a practitioner of literature but also because he is the man he is, the statement that his lecture has this purport will be shocking and perhaps it will be thought scarcely credible. And I have no doubt that, in another mood and on some other occasion, Sir Charles would be happy to assert the beneficent powers of literature. But there can be no other interpretation of his lecture than that it takes toward literature a position of extreme antagonism.

The Two Cultures begins as an objective statement of the lack of communication between scientists and literary men. This is a circumstance which must have been often observed and often deplored. Perhaps nothing in our culture is so characteristic as the separateness of the various artistic and intellectual professions. As between, say, poets and painters, or musicians and architects, there is very little discourse, and perhaps the same thing could be remarked of scientists of different interests, biologists and physicists, say. But the isolation of literary men from scientists may well seem to be the most extreme of these separations, if only because it is the most significant, for a reason which Sir Charles entirely understands: the especially close though never fully defined relation of these two professions with our social and political life.

The even-handedness with which Sir Charles at first describes the split between the two "cultures" does not continue for long. He begins by telling us that scientists and literary men are equally to blame for the separation—they are kept apart by "a gulf of mutual incomprehension," by distorted images of each other which give rise to dislike and hostility. But as Sir Charles's lecture proceeds, it becomes plain that, although the scientists do have certain crudities and limitations, they are in general in the right of things and the literary men in the wrong of them. The matter which causes the scales to shift thus suddenly is the human condition. This, Sir Charles tells us, is of its nature tragic: man dies, and he dies alone. But the awareness of the ineluctably tragic nature of human life makes a moral trap, "for it tempts one to sit back, complacent in one's unique tragedy," paying no heed to the circumstances of everyday life, which, for the larger number of human beings, are painful. It is the literary men, we are told, who are the most likely, the scientists who are the least likely, to fall into this moral trap; the scientists "are inclined to be impatient to see if something can be done: and inclined to think that it can be done, until it's proved otherwise." It is their spirit, "tough and good and determined to fight it out at the side of their brother men," which has "made scientists regard the other [i.e., the literary] culture's social attitudes as contemptible."

"This is too facile," Sir Charles says in mild rebuke of the scientists, by which he of course means that essentially they are right. There follows a brief consideration of a question raised not by Sir Charles in his own person but by "a scientist of distinction" whom he quotes. "Yeats, Pound, Wyndham Lewis, nine out of ten of those who have dominated literary sensibility in our time, weren't they not only politically silly, but politically wicked? Didn't the influence of all they represent bring Auschwitz that much nearer?" And Sir Charles in answer grants that Yeats was a magnanimous man and a great poet, but he will not, he says, defend the indefensible—"the facts . . . are broadly true." Sir Charles in general agrees, that is, that the literary sensibility of our time brought Auschwitz nearer. He goes on to say that things have changed considerably in the literary life in recent years, even if slowly, for "literature changes more slowly than science."

From the mention of Auschwitz onward, the way is open to the full assertion by Sir Charles of the virtues of the scientist. Although they are admitted to be sometimes gauche or stupidly self-assertive, although Sir Charles concedes of some of them that "the whole literature of the traditional culture doesn't seem relevant to [their] interests" and that, as a result, their "imaginative understanding" is diminished, he yet finds scientists to be men of a natural decency; they are free from racial feelings, they are lovers of equality, they are cooperative. And chief among their virtues, as Sir Charles describes them, is the fact that they "have the future in their bones."

Indeed, it turns out that it is the future, and not mere ignorance of each other's professional concerns, that makes the separation between the culture of science and the culture of literature. Scientists have the future in their bones. Literary men do not. Quite the contrary—"If the scientists have the future in their bones, then the traditional culture responds by wishing that the future did not exist." The future that the scientists have in their bones is understood to be nothing but a good future; it is very much like the history of the Marxists, which is always the triumph of the right, never possibly the record of defeat. In fact, to entertain the idea that the future might be bad is represented as being tantamount to moral ill-will—in a note appended to the sentence I have just quoted, Sir Charles speaks of George Orwell's *1984* as "the strongest possible wish that the future shall not exist."

It is difficult to credit the implications of this astonishing remark and to ascribe them to Sir Charles. As everyone recalls, Orwell's novel is an imagination of the condition of the world if the authoritarian tendencies which are to be observed in the present develop themselves—logically, as it were—in the future, the point being that it is quite within the range of possibility that this ultimate development should take place. In Orwell's representation of an absolute tyranny, science has a part, and a polemical partisan of science might understand this as the evidence of a literary man's malice toward science. But it is much more likely that, when Orwell imagined science as one of the instruments of repression, he meant to say that science, like everything else that is potentially good, like literature itself, can be perverted and debased to the ends of tyranny. Orwell was a man who, on the basis of actual and painful experience, tried to tell the truth about politics, even his own politics. I believe that he never gave up his commitment to socialism, but he refused to be illusioned in any way he could prevent; it lay within the reach of his mind to conceive that even an idealistic politics, perhaps especially an idealistic politics, can pervert itself. We must be puzzled to know what can be meant when such a man is said to entertain the strongest possible wish that the future shall not exist.

Having characterized the culture of literature, or, as he sometimes calls it, "the traditional culture," by its hostility to the future, Sir Charles goes on to say that "it is the traditional culture, to an extent remarkably little diminished by the emergence of the scientific one, which manages the Western world." This being so, it follows that the traditional culture must be strictly dealt with if the future is to be brought into being: what is called "the existing pattern" must be not merely changed but "broken." Only if this is done shall we be able to educate ourselves as we should. As for the need to educate ourselves: "To say, we have to educate ourselves or perish is perhaps a little more melodramatic than the facts warrant. To say, we have to educate ourselves or watch a steep decline in our lifetime is about right." And Sir Charles indicates our possible fate by the instance— he calls it a "historical myth"—of the Venetian Republic in its last half-century:

Its citizens had become rich, as we did, by accident. They had acquired immense political skill, just as we have. A good many of them were tough-minded, realistic, patriotic men. They knew, just as clearly as we know, that the current of history had begun to flow against them. Many of them gave their minds to working out ways to keep going. It would have meant breaking the pattern into which they had been crystallized. They were fond of the pattern, just as we are fond of ours. They never found the will to break it.

I quoted without comment Sir Charles's statement of the idea on which, we may say, the whole argument of *The Two Cultures* is based: "It is the traditional culture, to an extent remarkably little diminished by the emergence of the scientific one, which manages the Western world." It is a bewildering statement. In what way can we possibly understand it? That the Western world is managed by some agency which is traditional is of course comprehensible. And we can take in the idea that this agency may be described, for particular purposes of explanation, in terms of a certain set of mind, a general tendency of thought and feeling which, being pervasive, is hard to formulate, and that this is to be called a "culture." But for Sir Charles the words "traditional" and "literary" are interchangeable, and that this culture, as we agree to call it, is *literary,* that it bears the same relation to actual literary men and their books that what is called the "scientific culture" bears to scientists and their work in laboratories, is truly a staggering thought. The actions of parliaments and congresses and cabinets in directing the massive affairs of state, the negotiations of embassies, the movement of armies and fleets, the establishment of huge scientific projects for the contrivance of armaments and of factories for the production of them, the promises made to citizens, and the choices made by voters at the polls—these, we are asked to believe, are in the charge of the culture of literature. Can we possibly take this to be so?

It can of course be said that literature has some part in the management of the Western world, a part which is limited but perhaps not wholly unimportant. If, for example, we compare the present condition of industrial England with the condition of industrial England in the early nineteenth century, we can say that the present condition is not, in human respects, anything like what men of good will might wish it to be, but that it is very much better than it was in the early years of the Industrial Revolution. And if we then ask what agencies brought about the improvement, we can say that one of them was literature. Certain literary men raised the "Condition of England Question" in a passionate and effective way and their names are still memorable to us—Coleridge, Carlyle, Mill (I take him to be a man of letters; he was certainly a good literary critic), Dickens, Ruskin, Arnold, William Morris. They made their effect only upon individuals, but the individuals they touched were numerous, and by what they said they made it ever harder for people to be indifferent to the misery around them or to the degradation of the national life in which they came to think themselves implicated. These literary men helped materially, some would say decisively, to bring about a change in the state of affairs. This is not exactly management, but it is a directing influence such as literature in the modern time often undertakes to have and sometimes does have.

Yet in Sir Charles's opinion this directing influence of the literary men of the nineteenth century deserves no praise. On the contrary, his description of their work is but another count in the indictment of the culture of literature. Speaking of the response which literary men made to the Industrial Revolution, he says:

Almost everywhere . . . intellectual persons did not comprehend what was happening. Certainly the writers didn't. Plenty of them shuddered away, as though the right course for a man of feeling was to contract out; some, like Ruskin and William Morris and Thoreau and Emerson and Lawrence, tried various kinds of fancies, which were not much in effect more than screams of horror. It is hard to think of a writer of high class who really stretched his imaginative sympathy, who could see at once the hideous back-streets, the smoking chimneys, the internal price—and also the prospects of life that were opening out for the poor. . . .

Nothing could be further from the truth. No great English writer of the nineteenth century, once he had become aware of the Industrial Revolution, ever contracted out. This is not the place to rehearse the miseries that were acquiesced in by those who comforted the world and their own consciences with the thought of "the prospects of life that were opening out for the poor." It is enough to say that there were miseries in plenty of a brutal and horrifying kind, by no means adequately suggested by phrases like "the hideous back-streets, the smoking chimneys, the internal price." (Auschwitz, since it has been mentioned, may be thought of as the development of the conditions of the factories and mines of the earlier Industrial Revolution.) If the writers "shuddered away," it was not in maidenly disgust with machines and soot; if they uttered "screams of horror," it was out of moral outrage at what man had made of man—and of women and little children. Their emotions were no different from those expressed by Karl Marx in his chapter on the working day, nor from those expressed in Blue Books by the factory inspectors, those remarkable men of the middle class whom Marx, in a moving passage of *Capital,* praises and wonders at for their transcendence of their class feelings.

I have mentioned Matthew Arnold among those writers who made the old conditions of the Industrial Revolution ever less possible. Like many of his colleagues in this undertaking, he did entertain "fancies"—they all found modern life ugly and fatiguing and in some way false, and they set store by certain qualities which are no doubt traditional to the point of being archaic. But Arnold's peculiar distinction as a literary critic is founded on the strong sensitivity of his response to the modern situation. He uniquely understood what Hegel had told the world, that the French Revolution marked an absolute change in the condition of man. For the first time in history, Hegel said, Reason—or Idea, or Theory, or Creative Imagination—had become decisive in human destiny. Arnold's argument in "Literature and Science" was the affirmation of the French Revolution; he was speaking on behalf of the illumination and refinement of that Reason by which man might shape the conditions of his own existence. This is the whole purport of his famous statement, "Literature is the criticism of life."

That saying used to have a rough time of it, perhaps because people found the word *criticism* narrow and dour and wished to believe that life was worthier of being celebrated than criticized. But less and less, I think, will anyone find the ground on which to quarrel with it. Whatever else we also take literature to be, it must always, for us now, be the criticism of life.

But it would seem to be precisely the critical function of literature that troubles Sir Charles. And perhaps that is why, despite all that he says about the need to educate ourselves, he does not make a single substantive proposal about education.

If we undertake to say what the purpose of modern education is, our answer will surely be suggested by Arnold's phrase, together with the one by which he defined the particular function of criticism: "to see the object as in itself it really is." Whenever we undertake to pass judgment on an educational enterprise, the import of these two phrases serves as our criterion: we ask that education supply the means for a criticism of life and teach the student to try to see the object as in itself it really is. Yet when Sir Charles speaks of the need to break the "existing pattern" and to go on to the right education which will help us to establish the necessary new pattern, he does not touch upon any such standard of judgment. Although he would seem to be the likeliest person in the world to speak intelligently about the instruction in science of students who do not intend to be scientists, actually he says nothing more on the subject than that ignorance of the Second Law of Thermodynamics is equivalent to ignorance of Shakespeare, or that the Yang-Lee experiment at Columbia should have been a topic of general conversation at college High Tables.

Nor does he propose anything for the education of the scientist, except, of course, science. He does say that scientists need to be "trained not only in scientific but in human terms," but he does not say how. Scientists—but eventually one begins to wonder if they are really scientists and not advanced technologists and engineers—are to play a decisive part in the affairs of mankind, but nowhere does Sir Charles suggest that, if this is so, they will face difficulties and perplexities and that their education should include the study of books—they need not be "literary," they need not be "traditional": they might be contemporary works of history, sociology, anthropology, psychology, philosophy—which would raise the difficult questions and propose the tragic complexity of the human condition, which would suggest that it is not always easy to see the object as in itself it really is.

Well, it isn't beyond belief that a professional corps of high intellectual quality, especially if it is charged with great responsibility, should learn to ask its own questions and go on to make its own ethos, perhaps a very good one. But Sir Charles would seem to be asking for more than the right of scientists to go their own way. What he seems to require for scientists is the right to go their own way *with no questions asked*. The culture of literature, having done its worst, must now be supplanted; it is not even to play the part of a loyal opposition. How else are we to understand Sir Charles's belief in the endemic irresponsibility of the literary mind, his curious representation of the literary culture as having the management of the Western world, that is to say, as being answerable for all the anomalies, stupidities, and crimes of the Western world, for having made the "existing pattern" which must now be broken if the West is to survive or at least not suffer steep decline? It is manifest that the literary culture has lost the right to ask questions.

No one could possibly suppose of Charles Snow that he is a man who wants to curtail the rights of free criticism. The line which he takes in *The Two Cultures* is so far from the actuality of his temperament in this respect that we can only suppose that he doesn't mean it, not in all the extravagance of its literalness. Or we suppose that he means it at the behest of some large preoccupation of whose goodness he is so entirely convinced that he will seek to affirm it even in ways that would take him aback if the preoccupation were not in control of his thought. And this, I think, is the case. I believe that the position of *The Two Cultures* is to be explained by Sir Charles's well-known preoccupation with a good and necessary aim, with the assuring of peace, which is to say, with the compounding of the differences between the West and the Soviet Union. It is an aim which, in itself, can of course only do Sir Charles credit, yet it would seem to have implicit in it a strange, desperate method of implementing itself.

For the real message of *The Two Cultures* is that an understanding between the West and the Soviet Union could be achieved by the culture of scientists, which reaches over factitious national and ideological differences. The field of agreement would be the scientists' common perception of the need for coming together to put the possibilities of the scientific revolution at the disposal of the disadvantaged of all nations. The bond between scientists, Sir Charles has told us, is virtually biological: they all have the future in their bones. Science brings men together in despite of all barriers—speaking of the way in which the very wide differences in the social origins of English scientists were overcome to make the scientific culture of England (and seeming to imply that this is a unique grace of scientists, that English men of letters never had differences of social class to overcome), Sir Charles says, "Without thinking about it, they respond alike. That is what a culture means." And in the same way, "without thinking about it," the scientists of the West and the scientists of the Soviet Union may be expected to "respond alike." And, since "that is what a culture means," they will have joined together in an entity which will do what governments have not done, the work of relieving the misery of the world. But in the degree to which science naturally unites men, literature separates them, and the scientists of the world cannot form this beneficent entity until we of the West break the existing pattern of our traditional culture, the literary culture, which is self-regarding in its complacent acceptance of tragedy, which is not only indifferent to human suffering but willing to inflict it, which asks rude and impertinent questions about the present and even about the future.

It is a point of view which must, I suppose, in desperate days, have a show of reason. In desperate days, it always seems wise to throw something or someone overboard, preferably Jonah or Arion, the prophet or the poet. Mr. G. S. Fraser, for example, seems to understand what Sir Charles wants, and he is rather willing to go along with him, rather open to the idea that the achievement of peace may require some adverse judgment on literature. "It does not matter," he says, "whether we save the real Cambridge within the actual Cambridge . . . ; what we want to save is our actual human world with all the spots on it. This will not be done by teaching English at universities; men like Snow, at home both in Russia and America, and in a simple blunt way trying to teach these two blunt simple giants to understand each other, may in the end prove greater benefactors than Dr. Leavis."

No, the world will not be saved by teaching English at universities, nor, indeed, by any other literary activity. It is very hard to say what will save the world. But we can be perfectly certain that denying the actualities of the world will not work its salvation. Among these actualities politics is one. And it can be said of *The Two Cultures* that it communicates the strongest possible wish that we should forget about politics. It mentions national politics once, speaking of it as the clog upon the activity of scientists, as the impeding circumstance in which they must work. But the point is not developed and the lecture has the effect of suggesting that the issue is not between the abilities and good intentions of scientists and the inertia or bad will of governments; the issue is represented as being between the good culture of science and the bad culture of literature.

In this denial of the actuality of politics, Sir Charles is at one with the temper of intellectuals today—we all want politics not to exist, we all want that statement of Hegel's to be absolutely and immediately true, we dream of reason taking over the whole management of the world, and soon. No doubt a beneficent eventuality, but our impatience for it is dangerous if it leads us to deny the actuality of politics in the present. While we discuss, at Sir Charles's instance, the relative merits of scientific philosopher-kings as against literary philosopher-kings, politics goes on living its own autonomous life, of which one aspect is its massive resistance to reason. What is gained by describing the resistance to reason as other than it is, by thinking in the specious terms of two opposing "cultures"?

But of course the fact is that politics is not finally autonomous. It may be so massively resistant to reason that we are led to think of its resistance as absolute—in bad times we conceive politics to be nothing but power. Yet it cannot be said—at least not so long as politics relies in any degree upon ideology—that politics is never susceptible to such reason as is expressed in opinion, only that it is less susceptible in some nations and at some times than in other nations and at other times. And nowhere and at no time is politics exempt from moral judgment, whether or not that judgment is effectual. But if we make believe, as *The Two Cultures* does, that politics does not exist at all, then it cannot be the object of moral judgment. And if we deny all authority to literature, as *The Two Cultures* does, going so far as to say that this great traditional agency of moral awareness is itself immoral, then the very activity of moral judgment is impugned, except for that single instance of it which asserts the rightness of bringing the benefits of science to the disadvantaged of the world. In short, Sir Charles, seeking to advance the cause of understanding between the West and the Soviet Union, would seem to be saying that this understanding will come if we conceive both that politics cannot be judged (because it does not really exist) and that it should not be judged (because the traditional agency of judgment is irresponsible).

III

I take *The Two Cultures* to be a book which is mistaken in a very large way indeed. And I find the failure of Dr. Leavis's criticism of it to consist in his addressing himself not to the full extent of its error but to extraneous matters. From reading the Richmond Lecture one gains the impression that the substance of the Rede Lecture is extremely offensive to Dr. Leavis, that all his sensibilities are outraged by it: we conclude that Sir Charles wants something which is very different from what Dr. Leavis wants, and that Dr. Leavis thinks that what Sir Charles wants is crude and vulgar. But we can scarcely suppose from Dr. Leavis's response that what Sir Charles says has a very wide reference—for all we can tell, he might have been proposing a change in the University curriculum which Dr. Leavis is repelling with the violence and disgust that are no doubt often felt though not expressed at meetings of curriculum committees. For Dr. Leavis, who has always attached great importance to educational matters, the proposed change is certainly important beyond the University. He understands it both as likely to have a bad effect on the national culture and as being the expression of something already bad in the national culture. But this, we suppose, he would feel about any change in the curriculum.

In short, Dr. Leavis, in dealing with the Rede Lecture, has not seen the object as in itself it really is, just as Sir Charles, in dealing with the culture of literature in its relation to politics, has not seen the object as in itself it really is.

An example of the inadequacy of Dr. Leavis's criticism of *The Two Cultures* is his response to what Sir Charles says, in concert with that "scientist of distinction," about the political posture of the great writers of the modern period. That statement, if we stop short of its mention of Auschwitz—which makes a most important modification—certainly does have a color of truth. It is one of the cultural curiosities of the first three decades of the twentieth century that, while the educated people, the readers of books, tended to become ever more liberal and radical in their thought, there is no literary figure of the very first rank (although many of the next rank) who, in his work, makes use of or gives credence to liberal or radical ideas. I remarked on this circumstance in an essay of 1946. "Our educated class," I said, "has a ready if mild suspiciousness of the profit motive, a belief in progress, science, social legislation, planning, and international cooperation, perhaps especially where Russia is in question. These beliefs do great credit to those who hold them. Yet it is a comment, if not on our beliefs then on our way of holding them, that not a single first-rate writer has emerged to deal with these ideas, and the emotions that are consonant with them, in a great literary way. . . . If we name those writers who, by the general consent of the most serious criticism, by consent too of the very class of educated people of which we speak, are thought of as the monumental figures of our time, we see that to these writers the liberal ideology has been at best a matter of indifference. Proust, Joyce, Lawrence, Yeats, Mann [as novelist], Kafka, Rilke, Gide [also as novelist]—all of them have their own love of justice and the good life, but in not one of them does it take the form of a love of the ideas and emotions which liberal democracy, as known by our educated class, has declared respectable."

To which it can be added that some great writers have in their work given utterance or credence to conservative and even reactionary ideas, and that some in their personal lives have maintained a settled indifference to all political issues, or a disdain of them. No reader is likely to derive political light from either the works or the table talk of a modern literary genius, and some readers (of weak mind) might even be led into bad political ways.

If these writers are to be brought to the bar of judgment, anyone who speaks as their advocate is not, as Sir Charles says, defending the indefensible. The advocacy can be conducted in honest and simple ways. It is not one of these ways to say that literature is by its nature or by definition innocent. Literature is powerful enough for us to suppose that it has the capability of doing harm. But the ideational influence of literature is by no means always as direct as, for polemical purposes, people sometimes say it is. As against the dismay of Sir Charles and the distinguished scientist at the reactionary tendencies of modern literary geniuses, there is the fact that the English poets who learned their trade from Yeats and Eliot, or even from Pound, have notably had no sympathy with the social ideas and attitudes of their poetical masters.

Every university teacher of literature will have observed the circumstance that young people who are of radical social and political opinion are virtually never troubled by the opposed views or the settled indifference of the great modern writers. This is not because the young exempt the writer from dealing with the serious problems of living, or because they see him through a mere aesthetic haze. It is because they know—and quite without instruction—that, in D. H. Lawrence's words, they are to trust the tale and not the teller of the tale. They perceive that the tale is always on the side of their own generous impulses. They know that, if the future is in the bones of anyone, it is in the bones of the literary genius, and exactly because the present is in his bones, exactly because the past is in his bones. They know that if a work of literature has any true artistic existence, it has value as a criticism of life; in whatever complex way it has chosen to speak, it is making a declaration about the qualities that life should have, about the qualities life does not have but should have. They feel, I think, that it is simply not possible for a work of literature that comes within the borders of greatness *not* to ask for more energy and fineness of life, and, by its own communication of awareness, bring these qualities into being. And if, in their experience of such a work, they happen upon an expression of contempt for some idea which they have connected with political virtue, they are not slow to understand that it is not the idea in its ideal form that is being despised, but the idea as it passes current in specious form, among certain and particular persons. I have yet to meet the student committed to an altruistic politics who is alienated from Stephen Dedalus by that young man's disgust with political idealism, just as I have yet to meet the student from the most disadvantaged background who feels debarred from what Yeats can give him by the poet's slurs upon shopkeepers or by anything else in his inexhaustible fund of snobbery.

If ever a man was qualified to state the case for literature, and far more persuasively than I have done, it is Dr. Leavis. His career as a critic and a teacher has been devoted exactly to the exposition of the idea that literature presents to us "the possibilities of life," the qualities of energy and fineness that life might have. And it is, of course, the intention of the Richmond Lecture to say just this in answer to Sir Charles's indictment. Yet something checks Dr. Leavis. When it is a question of the defense, not of literature in general, but of modern literature, he puts into countervailing evidence nothing more than a passage in which Lawrence says something, in a wry and grudging way, on behalf of social equality. This does not meet the charge; against it Sir Charles might cite a dozen instances in which Lawrence utters what Sir Charles—and perhaps even Dr. Leavis himself—would consider "the most imbecile expressions of anti-social feeling."

There is only one feasible approach to the anti-social utterances of many modern writers, and that is to consider whether their expressions of anti-social feeling are nothing but imbecile. It is the fact, like it or not, that a characteristic cultural enterprise of our time has been the questioning of society itself, not its particular forms and aspects but its very essence. To this extreme point has the criticism of life extended itself. On the ways of dealing with this phenomenon, that of horror and dismay, such as Sir Charles's, is perhaps the least useful. Far better, it seems to me, is the effort to understand what this passionate hostility to society implies, to ask whether it is a symptom, sufficiently gross, of the decline of the West, or whether it is not perhaps an act of critical energy on the part of the West, an act of critical energy on the part of society itself—the effort of society to identify in itself that which is but speciously good, the effort to understand afresh the nature of the life it is designed to foster. I would not anticipate the answer, but these questions make, I am sure, the right way to come at the phenomenon.

It is not the way that Dr. Leavis comes at the phenomenon, despite his saying that the university study of literature must take its stand on "the intellectual-cultural frontier." Actually, when it is a question of the frontier, he prefers—it is an honorable preference—to remain behind it or to take a position at certain check-points. For example, of the two D. H. Lawrences, the one who descended from the social-minded nineteenth century and who did in some sort, affirm the social idea, and the other, at least equally important, for whom the condition of salvation was the total negation of society, Dr. Leavis can be comfortable only with the former. His commitment to the intellectual-cultural frontier is sincere but chiefly theoretical; he has, as is well know, sympathy with very few modern writers, and he therefore cannot in good grace come to their defense against Sir Charles's characterization of them.

Mr. Walter Allen, writing in the *New York Times Book Review* shortly after the publication of the Richmond Lecture and the *Spectator* letters attacking and defending it, accurately remarked on "the common areas of agreement" between Dr. Leavis and Sir Charles. "One would expect . . . that Snow would be sympathetic to Leavis's emphasis on the all-importance of the moral center of literature," Mr. Allen said. "Both have attacked experiment in literature. Neither of them, to put it into crude shorthand, are Flaubert-and-Joyce men." The similarities go further. In point of social background the two men are not much apart, at least to the untutored American eye. Both spring from the provincial middle class in one or another of its strata, and whatever differences there may have been in the material advantages that were available or lacking to one or the other, neither was reared in the assumption of easy privilege. From these origins they derived, we may imagine, their strong sense of quotidian actuality and a respect for those who discharge the duties it imposes, and a high regard for the domestic affections, a quick dislike of the frivolous and merely elegant. Neither, as I have suggested, has any least responsiveness to the tendencies of modern thought or literature which are existential or subversive. A lively young person of advanced tastes would surely say that if ever two men were committed to England, Home, and Duty, they are Leavis and Snow—he would say that in this they are as alike as two squares.

There is one other regard, an especially significant one, in which they are similar. This is their feeling about social class. One of the chief interests of Sir Charles's novels is their explicitness about class as a determinative of the personal life, and in this respect *The Two Cultures* is quite as overt as the novels—its scientists make a new class by virtue of their alienation from the old class attitudes, and Sir Charles's identification of literary men with the traditional culture which supposedly manages the Western world implies that they are in effect the representatives of an aristocratic ruling class, decadent but still powerful. The work of Dr. Leavis is no less suffused by the idea of social class, even though its preoccupation with the subject is far less explicit. To my recollection, Dr. Leavis does not make use of any of the words which denote the distinctions of English society— he does not refer to an aristocracy, a gentry, an upper middle or lower middle or working class. For him a class defines itself by its idea of itself—that is, by its tastes and style. Class is for him a cultural entity. And when he conceives of class power, as he often does, it is not economic or political power but, rather, cultural power that he thinks of. It is true that cultural power presents itself to his mind as being in some way suggestive of class power, but the actualities of power or influence are for him always secondary to the culture from which they arose or to which they give rise.

And indeed, no less than Sir Charles, Dr. Leavis is committed to the creation of a new class. This, we might even say, is the whole motive of his work. The social situation he would seem to assume is one in which there is a fair amount of mobility which is yet controlled and limited by the tendency of the mobile people to allow themselves to be absorbed into one of the traditional classes. As against the attraction exerted by a quasi-aristocratic, metropolitan upper middle class, Dr. Leavis has taken it to be his function to organize the mobile people, those of them who are gifted and conscious, into a new social class formed on the basis of its serious understanding of and response to literature, chiefly English literature. In this undertaking he has by no means been wholly unsuccessful. One has the impression that many of the students he has trained think of themselves, as they take up their posts in secondary schools and universities, as constituting at least a social cadre.

The only other time I wrote about Dr. Leavis I remarked that the

Cromwellian Revolution had never really come to an end in England and that Dr. Leavis was one of the chief colonels of the Roundhead party. His ideal readers are people who "are seriously interested in literature," and it is on their behalf that he wages war against a cultural-social class which, when it concerns itself with literature, avows its preference for the qualities of grace, lightness, and irony, and deprecates an overt sincerity and seriousness. "To a polished nation," said Gibbon, "poetry is an amusement of the fancy, not a passion of the soul," and all through his career it is against everything that Gibbon means by a polished nation and might mean by a polished class that Dr. Leavis has set his face. Bloomsbury has been his characteristic antagonist. But now, in Charles Snow, he confronts an opponent who is as Roundhead as himself, and as earnest and *intentional*.

To this confrontation Dr. Leavis is not adequate. It is not an adequate response to the massive intention of *The Two Cultures* for Dr. Leavis to meet Sir Charles's cultural preferences with his own preferences; or to seek to discredit Sir Charles's ideas chiefly by making them out to be vulgar ideas or outmoded ("Wellsian") ideas; or to offer, as against Sir Charles's vision of a future made happier by science, the charms of primitive peoples "with their marvellous arts and skills and vital intelligence." I do not mean to say that Dr. Leavis does not know where Sir Charles goes wrong in the details of his argument—he is as clear as we expect him to be in rebuking that large unhappy blunder about the Victorian writers. Nor, certainly, do I mean that Dr. Leavis does not know what the great fundamental mistake of Sir Charles's position is—he does, and he can be eloquent in asserting against a simplistic confidence in a scientific "future" the need of mankind, in the face of a rapid advance of science and technology, "to be in full intelligent possession of its full humanity (and 'possession' here means, not confident ownership of that which belongs to *us*—our property, but a basic living deference towards that to which, opening as it does into the unknown and itself immeasurable, we know we belong)." But such moments of largeness do not save the Richmond Lecture from its general parochialism. For example, of the almost limitless political implications of Sir Charles's position it gives no evidence of awareness. And if we undertake to find a reason for the inadequacy of Dr. Leavis's response, we will find, I think, that it is the same as the reason which accounts for Sir Charles having been in the first place so wholly mistaken in what he says—both men set too much store by the idea of *culture* as a category of thought.

The concept of culture is an idea of great attractiveness and undoubted usefulness. We may say that it begins in the assumption that all human expressions or artifacts are indicative of some considerable tendencies in the life of social groups or sub-groups, and that what is indicative is also causative—all cultural facts have their consequences. To think in cultural terms is to consider human expressions not only in their overt existence and avowed intention, but in, as it were, their secret life, taking cognizance of the desires and impulses which lie behind the open formulation. In the judgments which we make when we think in the category of culture we rely to a very large extent upon the style in which an expression is made, believing that style will indicate, or betray, what is not intended to be expressed. The aesthetic mode is integral to the idea of culture, and our judgments of social groups are likely to be made chiefly on an aesthetic basis—we like or do not like what we call their lifestyles, and even when we judge moralities, the criterion by which we choose between two moralities of, say, equal strictness or equal laxness is likely to be an aesthetic one.

The concept of culture affords to those who use it a sense of the liberation of their thought, for they deal less with abstractions and mere objects, more with the momentous actualities of human feelings as these shape and condition the human community, as they make and as they indicate the quality of man's existence. Not the least of the attractions of the cultural mode of thought are the passions which attend it—because it assumes that all things are causative or indicative of the whole of the cultural life, it proposes to us those intensities of moralized feeling which seem appropriate to our sense that all that is good in life is at stake in every cultural action. An instance of mediocrity or failure in art or thought is not only what it is but also a sin, deserving to be treated as such. These passions are no doubt vivifying: they have the semblance of heroism.

And if we undertake to say what were the circumstances that made the cultural mode of thought as available and as authoritative as it now is, we must refer to Marx, and to Freud, and to the general movement of existentialism, to all that the tendencies of modernity imply of the sense of contingency in life, from which we learn that the one thing that can be disputed, and that is worth disputing, is preference or taste. The Rede Lecture and the Richmond Lecture exemplify the use to which the idea of culture can be put in shaking the old certainties of class, in contriving new social groups on the basis of taste.

All this does indeed give the cultural mode of thought a very considerable authority. Yet sometimes we may wonder if it is wholly an accident that so strong an impulse to base our sense of life, and conduct of the intellectual life, chiefly upon the confrontations of taste should have developed in an age dominated by advertising, the wonderful and terrible art which teaches us that we define ourselves and realize our true being by choosing the right style. In our more depressed moments we might be led to ask whether there is a real difference between being the Person Who defines himself by his commitment to one or another idea of morality, politics, literature, or city-planning, and being the Person Who defines himself by wearing trousers without pleats.

We can, I suppose, no more escape from the cultural mode of thought than we can escape from culture itself. Yet perhaps we must learn to cast a somewhat colder eye upon it for the sake of whatever regard we have for the intellectual life, for the possibility of rational discourse. Sir Charles envisages a new and very powerful social class on the basis of a life-style which he imputes to a certain profession in contrast with the life-style he imputes to another profession, and he goes on from there to deny both the reality of politics and the possibility of its being judged by moral standards. Dr. Leavis answers him with a passion of personal scorn which obscures the greater part of the issue and offers in contradiction truth indeed but truth so hampered and hidden by the defenses of Dr. Leavis's own choice in life-styles that it looks not much different from a prejudice. And the *Spectator* correspondents exercise their taste in life-styles and take appropriate sides. It is at such a moment that our dispirited minds yearn to find comfort and courage in the idea of mind, that faculty whose ancient potency our commitment to the idea of culture denies. To us today, mind must inevitably seem but a poor gray thing, for it always sought to detach itself from the passions (but not from the emotions, Spinoza said, and explained the difference) and from the conditions of time and place. Yet it is salutary for us to contemplate it, whatever its grayness, because of the bright belief that was once attached to it, that it was the faculty which belonged not to professions, or to social classes, or to cultural groups, but to man, and that it was possible for men, and becoming to them, to learn its proper use, for it was the means by which they could communicate with each other.

It was on this belief that science based its early existence, and it gave to the men who held it a character which is worth remarking. Sir Charles mentions Faraday among those scientists who overrode the limitations of social class to form the "scientific culture" of England. This is true only so far as it can be made consonant with the fact that Faraday could not have imagined the idea of a "scientific culture" and would have been wholly repelled by it. It is told of Faraday that he refused to be called a *physicist;* he very much disliked the new name, as being too special and particular, and insisted on the old one, *philosopher,* in all its spacious generality: we may suppose that this was his way of saying that he had not overridden the limiting conditions of class only to submit to the limitations of profession. The idea of mind which had taught the bookbinder's apprentice to embark on his heroic enterprise of self-instruction also taught the great scientist to place himself beyond the specialness of interest which groups prescribe for their members. Every personal episode in Tyndall's classic account of his master, *Faraday as a Researcher,* makes it plain that Faraday undertook to be, in the beautiful lost sense of the word, a *disinterested* man. From his belief in mind, he derived the certitude that he had his true being not as a member of this or that profession or class, but as—in the words of a poet of his time—"a man speaking to men."

No one now needs to be reminded of what may befall the idea of mind in the way of excess and distortion. The literature of the nineteenth century never wearied of telling us just this, of decrying the fatigue and desiccation of spirit which result from an allegiance to mind that excludes impulse and will, and desire and preference. It was, surely, a liberation to be made aware of this, and then to go on to take serious account of those particularities of impulse and will, of desire and preference, which differentiate individuals and groups—to employ what I have called the cultural mode of thought. We take it for granted that this, like any other mode of thought, has its peculiar dangers, but there is cause for surprise and regret that it should be Sir Charles Snow and Dr. Leavis who have jointly demonstrated how far the cultural mode of thought can go in excess and distortion.

Hawthorne in Our Time

HENRY JAMES'S monograph on Hawthorne must always have a special place in American letters if only because, as Edmund Wilson observed, it is the first extended study ever to be made of an American writer. But of course it is kept in the forefront of our interest by more things than its priority. We respond to its lively sense of the American cultural existence and the American cultural destiny, to the vivacity which arises from James's happy certitude that, in describing the career of the first fully developed American artist, he celebrates the founder of a line in which he himself is to stand pre-eminent. And we can scarcely fail to be captivated by the tone of James's critical discourse, of a mind informed and enlightened, delighting in itself and in all comely and civilized things; it is the tone of the center, far removed from the parochialism which (together with strength) James imputes to Poe as a critic. For the student of American literature in general the little book is indispensable.

But the student of American literature for whom Hawthorne is a particular concern must experience some degree of discomfort as he reads James on his author. He will be aware that through James's high and gracious praise there runs a vein of reserve, even of condescension. In an attempt to account for this, the student will perhaps reflect that Hawthorne made himself susceptible to condescension, for he was often at pains to avow the harmlessness of his temperament, to dissociate himself from the fierce aggressions and self-assertions of the literary life; he seems to ask from his readers a tender and cherishing affection rather than the stern regard which we give to the more violent or demonic personalities—or, simply, to the personalities more overtly masculine—whose assault upon us we learn to forgive. Then too, it is not hard to understand that James, in the full pride of his still youthful powers, might have been tempted to slight a predecessor, no matter how truly admired—a predecessor who, although he did indeed show how much could be accomplished in the way of art, did not achieve a body of work which, in bulk and fierce affronting power, equals that which his successor planned for himself in sublime confidence.

But when our student of Hawthorne has canvassed the reasons to be found in the personal circumstances of either man, he is bound to see that something beyond the personal is at work to produce James's reserve or condescension. He will understand that his explanation must ultimately refer to a cultural assumption to which James has given expression. And this assumption, when he examines it, will force upon him the awareness that, in the degree that he feels close to Hawthorne, the breach between his own contemporary culture and that of Henry James is very great. James's little book appeared (in the *English Men of Letters* series) in 1879, and in the time between then and now there has taken place a revision of critical sensibility the extent of which can scarcely be overestimated.

In his third chapter, which deals with *Mosses from an Old Manse* and *Twice-Told Tales,* James set forth his view of the nature of Hawthorne's artistic enterprise by taking issue with the opinion of Emile Montégut, an able French critic, notable to us for his special and informed interest in American literature. In 1860, in an essay called "Un romancier pessimiste," Montégut had dealt extensively with Hawthorne, representing him as a writer of dark and, indeed, misanthropic mind. He spoke at length of Hawthorne's concern with conscience, sin, and hell, and with "the tortures of a heart closed before man and open to God," subjects for which the descendant of a long line of Puritans would naturally show a predilection.

Montégut has but little sympathy to give to the Puritan mentality and he speaks in harsh terms of what he takes to be Hawthorne's exemplification of it, yet it is clear that he understands Hawthorne's dark preoccupation to constitute his chief interest, the very substance of his seriousness. To this view James responds with extreme and satiric impatience. He denies the darkness of Hawthorne's mind and in the course of doing so actually seems to deny that it is a serious mind. For he tells us that we must understand Hawthorne's concern with conscience to be largely "ironical." He does not use the adjective in the sense which will occur most naturally to the reader of today, the sense which is cognate with "ambiguous" and suggests a source of emotional power. He intends a meaning of the word which is close to whimsical playfulness. "He is to a considerable extent ironical—this is part of his charm—part, even, one may say, of his brightness; but he is neither bitter nor cynical, he is rarely even what I should call tragical." And James goes on: "There have certainly been story-tellers of a gayer and lighter spirit; there have been observers more humorous, more hilarious—though on the whole Hawthorne's observation has a smile in it oftener than may at first appear; but there has rarely been an observer more serene, less agitated by what he sees, and less disposed to call things deeply into question."

To the religious elements of the stories James gives no credence beyond an aesthetic one. Hawthorne, he says, used religion for his own artistic purposes; from the moral life of Puritanism his imagination "borrowed" a "color" and "reflected" a "hue," but he experienced no conviction whatever. James certainly abates nothing in his description of the terrors of Puritanism, of how the "shadow of the sense of sin" could darken the individual life and lead it either to despair or to a catastrophic rebellion. But he is quite certain that Hawthorne was not adversely affected by his Puritan heritage—he did not "groan and sweat and suffer" under it, nor did he throw it off in anger. ". . . He contrived by an exquisite process, best known to himself, to transmute this heavy moral burden into the very substance of his imagination, to make it evaporate in the light and charming fumes of artistic production."

James is unequivocal and emphatic in his belief that Hawthorne's interest in Puritanism was nothing but artistic. He tells us that our author gave his imagination license to "amuse" itself with the faith of his ancestors, to make their morality its "playground"; what for his forebears was the principle of existence, he made into one of his "toys." "The old Puritan moral sense, the consciousness of sin and hell, of the fearful nature of our responsibilities and the savage character of our Taskmaster—these things had been lodged in the mind of a man of Fancy, whose fancy had straightway begun to take liberties and play tricks with them—to judge them (Heaven forgive him!) from the poetic and aesthetic point of view, from the point of view of irony and entertainment." James has no quarrel with fancy, but he adheres to the Coleridgean doctrine that it is a lesser faculty than the imagination, and although he does not doubt that it is within Hawthorne's capacity to command the imagination, he understands the tales to be chiefly under the control of fancy. ". . . As a general thing," he says, "I should characterize the more metaphysical of our author's short stories as graceful and felicitous conceits."

What are we to do with a judgment of this sort—how are we to escape its embarrassments? It is one of our great masters who speaks, and we hold him to be great not only in the practice of his art but also in its theory. From him many of us learned how high, even sacred, is the mission of the artist, and from him we derived many of the tenets by which we judge success in art. Yet it is he who makes this estimate of another of our masters, the one who, of all Americans, was the master of Henry James himself.

I need scarcely detail the ways in which, by our modern judgment, James goes wrong. Yet it will be well to have the prevailing present view explicitly before us, and it could not be more exactly defined than by the existence of the useful volume called *A Casebook on the Hawthorne Question* (1962). The editor of the *Case-*

book, Professor Agnes Donohue, has gathered together ten of Hawthorne's best-known stories; to each of six of these she has appended two interpretative essays of more or less recent date; following this is a selection of famous critical estimates of our author; and in a series of appendices which includes lists of critical topics for student papers there is a bibliography which, although it is intended to be minimal, runs to thirty-two books and the same number of articles. Why it is that Hawthorne makes a "question" for us and how our literary community has gone about answering what has been posed to us is very clearly explained by the editor in her preface.

The ten stories and sketches in the Casebook disclose a signal ambiguity in Hawthorne—his attitude toward man's moral nature. Sometimes he seems to assert the depravity of man while at the same time he dreams of an Adamic hero guileless in his prelapsarian Eden. He vacillates between trusting the human heart's intuitions as good and advancing his conviction that the heart is a "foul cavern" which must be destroyed to be purified.

Hawthorne's ambivalence about guilt and innocence can be seen as a lodestone that draws into its magnetic field other problems of human life. He writes of innocents initiated into shrewdness; secret sin and isolation; compulsive rituals of atonement and sacrifice; self-righteousness becoming fanaticism; science confronting original sin; witchcraft and devil worship; carnal knowledge and guiltless love; the search for a home, a father, a self—in short, man's dark odyssey in an alien world.

The ambiguity in Hawthorne's stories is at once his triumph and, for some literalist critics, his failure. The tension it creates is a dramatic asset. Many of the tales or romances, as he thought of them, are multileveled, ironic explorations of the human psyche—capable of endless extensions of meaning and of stimulating repeated analysis and interpretation.

Comparing the two views of Hawthorne, that of James and the established modern view which Professor Donohue summarizes, we must, in all humility, feel that ours is the right one, or at least, for us, the inevitable one. It recommends itself on its face. No doubt James's ironical entertainer makes a graceful and charming figure as he amuses himself with the toys strewn over the playground of a disused morality. But how can any member of the literary community fail to conclude that there is an intrinsic superiority in the grave, complex, and difficult Hawthorne we have learned to possess, the Hawthorne who tells us about (to use Professor Donohue's phrase) "man's dark odyssey in an alien world"?

It is, of course, fair to remember that the view of himself that Hawthorne took was ostensibly more in accord with James's view of him than with ours. He was at pains to insist on the perspicuity of what he wrote: "The sketches are not, it is hardly necessary to say, profound; it is rather more remarkable that they so seldom, if ever, show any design on the writer's part to make them so. They have none of the abstruseness of idea, or obscurity of expression, which mark the written communications of a solitary mind with itself. They never need translation. . . . Every sentence, so far as it embodies thought and sensibility, may be understood and felt by anybody who will give himself the trouble to read it, and will take up the book in a proper mood."

To which the modern student of Hawthorne will say that his author is a foxy fellow indeed, and go on to explain what "read" really means, what is the extent of the necessary "trouble" that the reader will have to give himself, and what constitutes the "proper mood" in which the book is to be taken up. It is no secret how we achieved our modern Hawthorne, our dark poet, charged with chthonic knowledge, whose utterances are as ambiguous as those of any ancient riddling oracle, multi-leveled and hidden and "capable of endless extensions of meaning and of stimulating repeated analyses and interpretations"—it is plain that the Hawthorne of our day came into being at the behest of the famous movement of criticism that began some forty years ago, that movement of criticism which James could know nothing of, although he was to be one of its pre-eminent subjects.

And if we undertake to say how the critical movement put us in possession of our Hawthorne, we cannot be content to describe the process only in terms of the good effects of "close reading." The techniques of investigation and pedagogy which were employed by the critical movement are of manifest importance, but an understanding of modern criticism in its historical actuality requires that we be aware of an intention which is anterior to every technique. That intention was to give literature a new force and authority. Or perhaps we should say that the intention was to support the new degree of force and authority that literature was claiming for itself. The technical methods of modern criticism are summed up for us in the famous footnote in which Mr. Eliot told us that the spirit killeth but the letter giveth life. But by this statement Mr. Eliot meant something more than that the enlightened reader must pay strict attention to the minute details of literary art, or that criticism is not to be thought of as the adventures of a soul among masterpieces. He was making a statement about the nature of literature. We may understand him to have been saying that literature is of a *primitive* nature. For although the allegiance to "the letter" which he urged upon us will at first glance suggest intellectuality, and an intellectuality of a rather haughty sort, and something like a scientist glorification of precision, qualities which the critical movement in general does indeed often seem to claim for itself, it is actually an expression of belief in the magical force and authority of words and their arrangement, as in a charm or spell, an expression of belief that literature characteristically makes its appeal to archaic human faculties which have been overlaid by civilization and deeply hidden.

My reference to its belief in the "primitive" nature of literature will tell us only a little about the very large and very complex intention of modern criticism. But it may serve to remind us that the critical movement, in its diverse groups and parties, set itself up in opposition to what a social psychologist has called the "respect revolution" of our time. The phrase refers to the culture of democratic-capitalist industrialism and to that culture's devaluation of certain traditional ideas, modes of life, personnels, qualities of art, etc. The conception of art as "primitive," as taking its rise in an older mode of life, may be thought of as a way of challenging those aspects of the "respect revolution" which were rationalistic, positivistic, vulgar, and concerned with superficial and transitory rather than with deep and permanent things.

The phrase I have borrowed, awkward and jargonistic as it is, may serve to propose the thought that cultural impulses stand in the closest proximity to social impulses and are often scarcely to be distinguished from them—to speak of the "respect revolution" may remind us that a strong cultural preference has much in common with social antagonism.[1] The translation of modes of thought and of artistic imagination into modes of social antagonism, or the other way around, is natural and inevitable in our day, and of course it was practiced by the members of the critical movement itself. Everyone is aware of how important in his thought about poetry Mr. Eliot's social and political ideas were; in America many practitioners of the New Criticism took positions more or less like Mr. Eliot's, and the instance of Dr. Leavis reminds us that within the movement—which is by no means to be thought of as wholly defined by the work of the New Critics—there were sharp antagonisms of social preference, although at this distance in time the differences between one party and another are perhaps already of less importance than the antagonism which all parties showed to the social values that had been established by the respect revolution.[2]

The social emotions which were involved in the critical movement do not in themselves immediately concern us, but I mention

[1] An example which, although it is not drawn from the critical movement, is relevant to our subject is V. L. Parrington's representation of Hawthorne as being virtually an enemy of the common people because of the delicacy of his art, his concern with the inner life and the problem of evil, and his coldness to the enthusiasms of Transcendentalism, which Parrington describes as "the revolutionary criticism that was eager to pull down the old temples to make room for nobler."

[2] In the social-psychological view, Dr. Leavis is presumably no less "aristocratic" than Mr. Eliot. At any rate, I am—I picked up the phrase "respect revolution" from an essay in which it is said that my volume *The Opposing Self* "defends an aristocratic attitude toward the respect revolution in terms of an implicit romantic notion of inner direction" (Arthur J. Brodbeck, "Values in *The Lonely Crowd:* Ascent or Descent of Man?," in *Culture and Character,* edited by Seymour Martin Lipset and Leo Lowenthal, 1962, p. 59).

them in order to suggest how charged with will, how deeply implicated in the bitter moralities of choosing among social styles, was the intellectual tendency that gave us the Hawthorne we know.

But if we do indeed owe our Hawthorne to the movement of criticism, it may be that our new possession is a little compromised by the somewhat fatigued reputation of criticism in recent years. In 1956, in his University of Minnesota lecture, Mr. Eliot expressed what he was not alone in feeling—a degree of disenchantment with the enormous critical activity of our age.[3] He was ready to affirm that our criticism was very brilliant, but he felt it necessary to say that "it may even come to seem, in retrospect, too brilliant." By which he meant, I think, too busy, too eager to identify ironies, and to point to ambiguities, and to make repeated analyses and interpretations.

One objection that Mr. Eliot made to the hyperactivity of criticism is that it interferes with our private and personal relation to the literary work, that it prevents our freedom to respond to it in our own way. I should go further than this and say that the brilliant busyness of criticism has not only changed our relation to literature, to art in general, but has even changed our conception of the nature of art, and in a way that, if we stop to think of it, we might not be entirely happy about.

The situation that I would describe is by way of being a paradox. Of this paradox the first term is our belief that the vulgar art-product, the art-product characteristic of the respect revolution, stands in a relation to the public which is radically different from the relation to the public maintained by the work that commands our best attention and admiration. The former, the "popular" or middlebrow work, consciously refers itself to the public and is shaped by its response to public prejudices and desires. The latter, the work of genius or disinterested talent, refers itself only to the inner life of its creator and is to be judged only by the truth of its

---

[3] I should here take note of Mr. Eliot's statement that the critical movement ought not to be thought of as deriving from him.

representation of that innerness. Our commitment to this criterion constitutes, as M. H. Abrams tells us, the basis of our modern aesthetic. In his admirable *The Mirror and the Lamp,* after describing the "mimetic" theories of art of classical antiquity and the "pragmatic" theories of the Renaissance and the eighteenth century, Professor Abrams goes on to speak of the "expressive" theories of our own time: "The first test any poem must pass is no longer, 'Is it true to nature?' or 'Is it appropriate to the requirements either of the best judges or the generality of mankind?' but a criterion looking in a different direction; namely, 'Is it sincere? Is it genuine? Does it match the intention, the feeling, and the actual state of mind of the poet while composing?' The work ceases then to be regarded as primarily a reflection of nature . . . the mirror held up to nature becomes transparent and yields the recorded insights into the mind and heart of the poet himself." This is in large part true, yet an accurate account of this first criterion of modern judgment must not lead us to believe that our response stops with our testing the congruity between the created work and its maker's inner life at the time of its creation. We must be aware that, once we have made our way into the artist's inner life in order to decide whether or not the created work is congruent with it, the artist's inner life ceases in some degree to be inner. It is on public view, available to general scrutiny and judgment.

The artist, of course, makes no objection to his innerness being thus publicized. If we consider the situation of the arts in general in Paris between 1885 and 1914, which is the definitive period of the modern epoch, we can say that it was characterized by the passionate devotion of the artists to their inner lives, to their personal and peculiar visions. But in all the history of art was there ever a movement which was so conscious of a public, even though in its deficiencies rather than in its legitimate expectations, and so determined to impose itself upon the public? The artist himself often led the enterprise of making his work prevail, but this was not necessary— when once its sincerity and genuineness were agreed upon by a faithful few, there gathered around the work a band of fighting men to carry it onto the field in force, like the Ark of the Covenant, each member of the band deriving strength from the sacred object, becoming ever more confirmed in his own sincerity and genuineness while bringing into ultimate question the authenticity of the heathen public.

Hence our paradox. Never, in a secular culture, has the inner life seemed of such moment as it does in our culture. And never has the inner life been lived so publicly, so much in terms of significant associations and allegiances, of admirations and rejections which make plain how things stand within.

As a result, it becomes ever more difficult for a work of art to be thought of as existing in itself or in our private and personal experience of it—its existence becomes the elaborate respect systems that grow up around it, that huge penumbra of the public effort to understand it and to be in a right relation to it, and to make known to the world the completeness of the understanding and the rightness of the relation that has been achieved. The work exists less in itself than in the purview of one or another of the public agencies we have set up for the service of the inner life. Of these one of the most notable is surely literary criticism, which, as it has established itself in the universities, constitutes a great new profession, ever growing in its personnel and in its influence.[4]

The extent of our author's public existence will not seem irrelevant to the Hawthorne Question (since there is such a thing), for Hawthorne's relation to the public of his own day was a matter of great moment in his thought about himself. Hawthorne seems never to have been sure whether to be ashamed or proud of his lack of success with the mass of his countrymen. And of course this was

---

[4] For an interesting account of the part played by public agencies—"museums, university art departments, professional publications"—in the establishment of new painting see Harold Rosenberg's column in *The New Yorker*, September 7, 1963, pp. 136–46. Mr. Rosenberg's estimate of the power—one might say the fury—of criticism is worth noting: "The future does not come about of itself; it is the result of choices and actions in the present. Criticism, including art criticism, is a form of conflict about what shall be. If history can make into art what is now not art, it can also unmake what is now art. It is conceivable that Michelangelo, Vermeer, Goya, Cézanne will someday cease to be art; it is only necessary that, as in the past, an extreme ideology shall seize power and cast out existing masterpieces as creatures of darkness."

not for him merely a question of his career but of his moral life, feeling as he did that to be removed from one's fellow beings was to commit a mortal sin. His ambivalence is expressed in the Preface to *Twice-Told Tales*. He tells us—it is touching to hear him say it— that the stories are written in "the style of a man of society," that they are "his attempt to open an intercourse with the world." Yet Hawthorne's impulse to privacy is definitive of his genius. We think so and he thought so. The delicate, the fragile, the evanescent, all that could not survive the public touch or gaze, made his conception of success in art. Of his tales he says that "they have the blue tint of flowers that blossomed in too retired a shade—the coolness of meditative habit which diffuses itself through the feeling and obser- vation of every sketch." The flower was for him the perfect symbol of the created work: he was at pains to revise his ancient family name so that it would be more precisely that of a beautiful flower- bearing tree, its blossoms delicate and brief, its integrity and isola- tion enforced by its spines or thorns.

It is all too possible that in having made Hawthorne public, in having busied ourselves to discover that he is a Question, which then we must bestir ourselves to answer, we have lost much of the charm and fragrance which may well be his essence. James was much engaged by the beauty of Hawthorne's work, by its textures and hues, of which he speaks not so much with critical admiration as with personal delight. Of this surface aesthetic the contemporary critics in Professor Donohue's volume say little. Their concern is with an aesthetic of depth, an aesthetic of the arrangement of quasi- doctrinal significances. One cannot have everything, but whoever has first read Hawthorne in childhood—James makes a point of his having done so—will be inclined to feel that something he once knew is missing, something that spoke to him, and very movingly, before ever ambiguity was a word, some wind or music of unpartic- ular significance that had its abode in the forests and haunted the Notch and played around the Great Stone Face.

It is a loss, but no doubt we must teach ourselves to sustain it cheerfully. For how else are we to deal with Hawthorne than in the public way we do deal with him? He belongs in the canon of our spiritual heritage, and how else is one to impart that heritage, how else is one to be a serious critic or a university teacher, if he is not as *active* as he may be in response to his subject? And if one perhaps goes on to think of his profession as having a more than pedagogic function, as being charged to make some contribution to the effort of spiritual discovery of our time, one may not surrender one's right to press each work as hard as one can in order to make it yield the full of its possible meaning.

Henry James's Hawthorne will not suit the purposes of the teacher or critic, neither his strictly professional nor his larger cultural and spiritual purposes. What can we do with a Hawthorne who, in dealing with the heavy moral burden which was his ancestral heritage, not only refused to accept it as his own but contrived to make it "evaporate in the light and charming fumes of artistic production," a sort of ethical prestidigitator?

I confess to being of the opinion that in establishing our Hawthorne as against Henry James's Hawthorne we have lost something of considerable value. But I am constrained to heed the contention that we have gained more than we have lost. I must even be aware that we have acquired an augmented canon. For us today none of Hawthorne's stories surpasses in interest "My Kinsman, Major Molineux." James does not mention this great story. And indeed it is only in relatively recent years that it presents itself as demanding inclusion in any selection of Hawthorne's work which might be made—when Austin Warren in 1938 and Newton Arvin in 1946 prepared selected editions of the tales, neither of the two editors, whose literary intelligence is of a very high order, included the story we have come especially to prize. Its Dionysian darkness, its brilliant, bitter, ambivalent humor, were presumably not yet available to them, not yet available to us.

Let us, then, stay confirmed in our belief that the Hawthorne we now have is the right one. But it may be worth asking why it is that

James's Hawthorne is so different from ours. I said earlier that James's view was not merely personal, that it was controlled by a cultural assumption. Remembering the year of the monograph, 1879, at the apogee of Victorianism, we are tempted to say that this assumption is part of the ideology of Philistinism which always hovered over even the best thought of the Victorian era. What we mean by Philistinism surely accommodates James's almost angry insistence that our author is not possibly to be thought of as dark or bitter or pessimistic, is not to be called "tragical," virtually not serious, that he is childlike in the indulgence of his fancy, that his only concern is to amuse himself and entertain us; and this is not to mention James's expressed dislike of "symbols and correspondences," of "seeing a story told as if it were another and very different story." James, of course, figures in our minds exactly as an avowed enemy of Philistinism, yet an ideology works in mysterious ways, no one can be sure of being immune from all its effects, and it may be that we have to admit that James was in accord with some of the questionable aspects of his epoch.

This unhappy possibility might be sustained by the recollection of a certain passage from *The Ambassadors,* the famous speech that Lambert Strether makes to Little Bilham. "Live all you can," Strether says to his young friend, "it's a mistake not to. It doesn't so much matter what you do in particular, so long as you have your life. If you haven't had that, what have you had? . . ." When, in the 1940s, James was in the full tide of the great revival of interest in him, this speech was frequently quoted. Twenty years ago the little homily seemed to touch the American consciousness in a very intimate way. *Live all you can; it's a mistake not to.* How much that seemed to say about America—our nation gave us much, but it was ever reluctant to grant us the right to have our lives. No one thought that the implied doctrine was the whole of James, yet it seemed very much at the center of his work, and its intensely asserted positivism validated him for many readers who might otherwise have been put off him, just as now, in a different cultural moment, it accounts, as I think, for much of that diminution of interest in James which is to be observed.[5]

What did James mean by having one's life? He meant something really quite simple and actual and tangible. He meant Paris—surely he meant that first. He meant all that was possible to do and enjoy in Paris and not in Woollett, Massachusetts—he meant having intense erotic relationships; and breaking the code of respectability without pain of conscience; and Gloriani's garden; and sunny days on the river; and Mme. de Vionnet's beauty and charm, and her manners and place in society. "To live" meant to know and to have the pleasures of the world.

James gave perfect credence to the pleasures of the world. He believed them to be real even at those moments when he was most intensely aware that they might be involved with vulgarity and even cruelty. He gave an equal credence to the sanctions which control and limit the ways in which the pleasures of the world may be seized, and to the moral sensibilities which propose the circumstances in which the pleasures of the world—perhaps the world itself—must be surrendered. The credence he gave to pleasure and the credence he gave to moral sanction together define James's certitude that the world is *there:* the unquestionable, inescapable world; the world so beautifully and so disastrously solid, physical, material, "natural."

And I think that it is because the world is so very much there for James that our interest in his work has receded from the high point it reached two decades ago. It does not move us now as it once did to hear him say, "Live as much as you can; it's a mistake not to." Whatever Paris and Gloriani's garden and a free and happy sexuality may mean to our practical consciousness (perhaps everything!), to our literary or spiritual consciousness they now mean but little. If we can imagine a novelist of our own moment who matched James

[5] I have in mind only the situation in America. In England, where James was never a public issue, he is very widely read, for simple purposes of delight, "for fun," as Jane Austen is, by people of the most diverse intellectual interests.

in genius, we cannot easily suppose that he would give anything like James's credence to the good "thereness" of the world, to the necessity of having one's life in the terms of the hedonism that James seems to celebrate. By the same token, we cannot easily suppose that he would give anything like James's credence to the moral sanctions which control and limit the ways in which the pleasures of the world may be grasped. These two credences, as I say, are the ground of James's art, constituting as they do his acceptance of the world's reality. They make the element of his work that tends to alienate it from the contemporary consciousness, that allows us to wonder whether we must not judge James to have been touched with the Philistinism of his epoch and therefore misled in his judgment of Hawthorne.[6]

Our contemporary feeling about the world, alien from that of James, is much in accord with that of Franz Kafka. Everything about Kafka is still in dispute, perhaps even more than it formerly was, now that our response to him has become more precise and discriminating. But almost everyone will agree that Kafka's work gives very little recognition, if any at all, to the world in its ordinary actuality, as it is the object of our desires and wills, as we know it socially, politically, erotically, domestically; or, if it recognizes the world at all, it does so only through what it perceives of the radical incompatibility of world and mankind. The lively little study of Kafka by Günther Anders seems to me especially satisfying because it responds so fully to Kafka as a *force,* speaking of him as a "dangerous" writer and questioning whether it is "wise" to admire him. Anders tells us that Kafka "provided exactly the mixture of sensation a certain class and generation of readers . . . most desired, pandering to their self-conscious sense of having reached the last phase of individualist sensibility. For here indeed were stories about the individual in his purest, most isolated role—yet told in a tone which showed how pointless was his position in the world. The

[6] It will perhaps save trouble if I explain that the sentence is ironic: I do not in literal fact think that James is properly to be called Philistine.

hero was still the center, but the center of complete indifference." In another passage, Anders speaks of Kafka's tone as transforming "men and things into a kind of *nature morte.*" The "class and generation of readers" which was given what it wanted by Kafka is said by Anders to be that which flourished in 1925. If this dating is accurate for Europe, it is not accurate for America, where Kafka, like James, made his strongest impression upon our literary culture in the '40s and continues to stand well to the fore of our interest while James recedes into the background.

The name of Kafka had to turn up sooner or later in any discussion of Hawthorne, for our awareness of the later man has done much to license our way of reading the earlier. Everyone perceives certain likenesses between Hawthorne and Kafka. They were similarly, although not equally, remote from the public, and to the public view they presented temperaments of which a defining element was a quality of personal gentleness at variance with the probing nature of their work. There is a very considerable degree of similarity in their preoccupations—"man's dark odyssey in an alien world" may serve to describe Kafka's as well as Hawthorne's. They stood in equivalent relations to religion: unbelievers both, their imaginations were captivated by the faiths to which they were connected by family tradition, and from these unavowed faiths they derived the license for the mythic genre which constitutes so much of their appeal, for the representation of agencies of human destiny which are not of the actual world. Then too, having in mind Kafka's negation of the world of actuality, I think it can fairly be said that there is something comparable in the way that Hawthorne deals with the world. He encourages the comparison when he tells us that he does not write novels but "romances," by which he means that his fiction does not make a very determined reference to the concrete substantialities of life, the observation and imitation of which is the definitive business of novels. We may surmise that his "simple" and "thinly-composed" society, as James called it, was congenial to his creative disposition, for it facilitated the enterprise that is characteristic of him, the representation of the world as being susceptible to penetration and suffusion by agencies not material and mundane. And it was exactly Hawthorne's happy acceptance of a thinly composed society that James jibbed at. He himself craved thickness; that famous list he drew up of the solid interesting actualities that were not at the disposal of Hawthorne's art, or the art of any American—"no Epsom, no Ascot!"—tells us, of course, what he was claiming for his own use when he transplanted himself to England, finding there, in its unassailable Britannic citadel, the Philistine solidity of world that he needed. And needed, one is inclined to say, not only as an artist but as a person—one has the sense that Hawthorne's art, because it represents a world which is only thinly composed, made James nervous.

What most troubled James in Hawthorne's work is not likely to trouble the reader who exercises the characteristic highly developed literary sensibility of our time. Indeed, as I have suggested, that modern reader is likely to find a measure of security in the very circumstance that made James anxious: in the degree that the world can be thought of as thinly composed, the autonomy of spirit is the more easily imagined.

But it is just here that we are likely to go astray in our perception of Hawthorne. For if it is indeed true that Hawthorne's world is thinly composed, we must yet see that whatever its composition lacks in thickness is supplied by an iron hardness. There are indeed similarities to be observed between Kafka and Hawthorne, but there is—after all, and despite first appearance—this decisive difference between them, that for Hawthorne the world is always and ineluctably *there* and in a very stubborn and uncompromising way. A passage in *The Marble Faun* tells us how perdurably Hawthorne understood it to be there. Kenyon, Hilda, and Miriam have been talking at length and fancifully about Count Donatello's resemblance to the antique statue of the dancing faun. "The foregoing conversation," we are told in that shameless explicit fashion that was once possible, "had been carried on in a mood in which all imaginative people, whether artists or poets, love to indulge. In this frame of mind, they sometimes find their profoundest truths side by side with the idlest jest, and utter one or the other apparently without distinguishing which is the most valuable, or assigning any considerable value to either. The resemblance between the marble faun and their living companion had made a deep half-serious, half-mirthful impression on these three friends, and had taken them into a certain airy region, lifting up, as it is so pleasant to feel them lifted, their heavy earthly feet from the actual soil of life. The world had been set afloat, as it were, for a moment, and relieved them, for just so long, of all the customary responsibility for what they thought and said." It is merely the conversation of "creative" persons that Hawthorne says he is describing, but we surmise that he would wish us to have in mind as well the works of art which they create, that he means to define the relation in which the artist stands to the world. If that is so, we will not fail to observe that what Hawthorne emphasizes in his account of this relation is not the power of the artistic imagination but the intractability of the world. For a brief moment the artist takes flight from it, and sometimes he can even seem to set the very world afloat; but only for so long as his words are being uttered; when again he falls silent, the world is no longer a balloon and his feet walk again on earth, on "the actual soil of life."

Of possible conceptions of the artist's relation to the world, this is indeed a very modest one. And if at any time in our judgment of Hawthorne we become aware, as indeed we must, of moments when his power as an artist seems insufficient to the occasion, we might reasonably attribute what weakness we discern in his art to a conception of the artist's manner of dealing with the world which is less bold and intransigent than it might be.

When it comes to power—to, as we say, sheer power—Hawthorne is manifestly inferior to Kafka. Of Kafka's power an impressive index is the fact that his version of man's dark odyssey proceeds without touching upon cases of conscience. In such relations between man and man as are represented in Kafka's work, it is never a possibility that one man can help or injure another. The idea "I did him wrong" is foreign to his mind. The idea "I did wrong" is of course omnipresent, but this means only "I did not do the required thing, that which the Law demands; and therefore I shall be punished." What an intransigence of imagination is needed to conceive man's spiritual life as having no discernible connection with morality! And not only its power is to be attributed to the intransigence of his imagination but also the extraordinary aesthetic success which Kafka consistently achieves. Aesthetically, it seems, it is impossible for him to fail. There is never a fault of conception or execution, never an error of taste, or logic, or emphasis. As why should there be? An imagination so boldly autonomous, once it has brought itself into being, conceives of nothing that can throw it off its stride. Like the dream, it confronts subjective fact only, and there are no aesthetically unsuccessful dreams, no failed nightmares.

The dream, it need scarcely be said, plays its part in the imagination of Hawthorne too, and most markedly in those of his works which touch us most deeply. But it is obvious that the "spontaneous, peremptory, and obligatory nature of dreaming"[7] manifests itself far less in Hawthorne than in Kafka. Over Hawthorne's imagination the literal actuality of the world always maintains its dominion. This must be kept to the forefront of our understanding of Hawthorne, even though we go on to say that he made it his characteristic enterprise to represent the moral life as existing beyond the merely pragmatic, to show it to us as a mystery, as being hidden, dark, and dangerous, and as having some part of its existence in a world which is not that of our ordinary knowledge. This other world, in which the presence of divinity is to be dimly apprehended, interpenetrates the world of material circumstance, and, in doing so, provides the quotidian and actual world with its most intense significances.

7 I take the phrase from the remarkable "Studies on the Psychopathology of Sleep and Dreams" by Charles Fisher, M.D., and William C. Dement, M.D., in *The American Journal of Psychiatry*, vol. 119, no. 12, June 1963, p. 1163.

When Hawthorne is successful in suggesting the interpenetration of the two worlds, he affects us profoundly. But we cannot fail to be aware of how readily his belief in the other unseen world can be checked by his sense of this world's actuality and intractability, how often it falls short of being spontaneous, peremptory, and obligatory. James's violent dislike of allegory and emblematic devices makes him unduly harsh in condemnation of the flaming celestial A in *The Scarlet Letter;* he judges the scene to be "not moral tragedy, but physical comedy." This is extreme, but we all agree to the principle of his objection and recall how much too often Hawthorne gave occasion for its being made. "Roger Malvin's Burial" may serve as our example of the characteristic weakness. The informing idea of this story is superb, and its execution is adequate to its conception up to the moment when we are asked to consider "whose guilt had blasted" the topmost bough of the oak, that withered bough which is to fall at the moment when Reuben Bourne has expiated his sin. Perhaps no other work of literature proposes so forcibly the idea that morality is not bounded by the pragmatic, that it creates a habitation for itself which is not only of this world, that it moves, by some process of transcendence, from practicality into absoluteness, or at least to unreasoning piety. The morality that Hawthorne has been conceiving has, as it were, the power of the dream, for it is indeed spontaneous, peremptory, and obligatory; but the incident of the falling bough, which is intended to enforce upon us the belief that the moral law has just these qualities as its defining attributes, is itself merely gratuitous; it seems scarcely the work of the imagination at all, rather of the author's will; so far from strengthening the credence we give to the preternatural world, it leads us to think that the author's own belief is seeking support.

Eventually Hawthorne lost all power of belief in the other world, and with it all power of creation. The last years of his life are terrible to contemplate. His labor seems to have been as devoted as it ever was, but he confronted white paper with the knowledge that nothing he now might put on it could have value. We have Kafka at hand to suggest the dreadfulness of the doom: it was as if Hawthorne's gift had been confiscated in punishment for some indiscernible sin, perhaps one that to all appearances was a virtue. "By 1860 he had worked himself dry," Edward H. Davidson tells us in the introduction to his edition of *Dr. Grimshawe's Secret,* one of the several gray chaotic efforts of the last period. "The 'present, the actual,' he confessed, was too pressing, and in *Grimshawe* he tried to write a sermon for his time without any of the moral insights which had been his special distinction in the years before he had gone to England."

Yet if we set aside the misery of the decline—that fate which must sometimes seem all too peculiarly American!—and set aside too the instances of aesthetic failure in the great period, we have to say that Hawthorne, even when he was not intimidated by the "present, the actual," must be found to lack the power of imagination which we expect him to have when we respond to the degree of power he actually does have. Despite the best efforts of the critics, the contemporary reader must always, I think, be somewhat disappointed by Hawthorne. With so much readiness to apprehend the dark, the unregenerate, and evil itself, why must he be so quick to modulate what he sees? He is capable of conceiving the terrible black veil that Mr. Hooper wears over his face, and of pointing to the guilt that we each incur and hide and long to reveal—why, having triumphed in the creation of the dread emblem, must he raise the question of whether the veil is not an egotism, an object of irony? His most famous single utterance loses its great potential force in its rhetoric of qualification: " 'Be true! Be true! Be true! Show freely to the world, if not your worst, yet some trait whereby the worst may be inferred!' " Why not, we ask, actually your worst? If it is correct to say with Professor Davidson that the "special distinction" of Hawthorne lies in his "moral insights," we are in effect saying that he was concerned to look into something that is there to be looked into, and for our time an investigation of objective reality cannot have the same imaginative freedom and force as an affirmation or a negation, which has only a subjective obligation. Hawthorne's vision of the moral life, although it does indeed reach in one direction to the transcendental or spiritual, reaches also in the other direction to the psychological, leading the reader to ask, "Is this true to the fact as I know it?" To the readers of Hawthorne's own time, the psychological observation of the novelist, especially when it discovered the dark and subversive elements of the mind, served as a liberation; but we are becoming inured to psychology—to the typical "highly developed" reader of our time, it does not bring the old liberation of surprise, and one may even detect in our literary opinion the belief that, insofar as it is a knowledge derived from observation and susceptible of being systematized, made into a science, it constricts rather than enlarges our imagination of man.[8] A critic whose interpretation of our author must always be listened to with especial respect has remarked of Hawthorne that he was concerned with sin only in its pragmatic aspect—"not sin," F. O. Matthiessen said, "but its consequences for human lives is Hawthorne's major theme." I would demur a little from this judgment, for I think that sin itself held a strong fascination for Hawthorne. But there can be no doubt that his awareness of the consequences of sin was never far distant from his concern with sin itself. In short, he always consented to the power of his imagination being controlled by the power of the world.

So far as James was able to perceive the submission to this control, he admired Hawthorne and made him one of the masters of his own art. His discomfort began, and his rather irritable condescension came into play, when he saw the control somewhat lessen and the signs of an assertion of autonomy appear, when Hawthorne moved toward imaginative intransigence. We reverse James's judgment. The modern consciousness requires that an artist have an imagination which is more intransigent than James could allow, more spontaneous, peremptory, and obligatory, which shall impose

---

[8] On the contemporary status of psychology, as well as on the contemporary status of "the world," see in Hans Jonas's *The Gnostic Religion* (revised edition, 1963) the Epilogue, "Gnosticism, Nihilism and Existentialism."

itself upon us with such unquestionable authority that "the actual" can have no power over us but shall seem the creation of some inferior imagination, that of mere convention and habit. Our modern piety is preoccupied by the ideal of the autonomous self, or at least of the self as it seeks autonomy in its tortured dream of metaphysical freedom. Hawthorne could indeed conceive of our longed-for autonomy, and to some considerable extent exemplify it in his art; and in the degree that he does so, he is our possession and invites us to try to possess him ever more intimately. Yet we cannot but be aware that he resists us who are of the modern dispensation, that his own piety is not committed where ours is.

There is an episode in Daniel Cory's recent book about Santayana[9] which suggests the nature of Hawthorne's piety as I comprehend it. Mr. Cory tells us how, as a young man, he could not understand why Santayana should have described *The Realm of Matter,* the first of the four volumes of *The Realms of Being,* as " 'essentially the work of a moralist,' " and, with a touch of impatience, Santayana said to him, " 'Don't you understand by now that the real object of piety is matter—or Nature, if you prefer. It is the idea of Might—the ineluctable Yahveh of the Hebrew, when this primitive notion has been freed of its local and superstitious accretions.' " And Mr. Cory goes on to say that "all his life Santayana had been convinced that the religious attitude of *respect for God* is at bottom the same thing as our sense of dependence on an efficacious but largely unfathomed 'background' of human experience. . . . When our naïve ideas of God or Nature have been stripped of their pictorial and emotional accretions, what we are left with is the defiant core of both these ideas: the ineradicable conviction of primordial Might that impinges upon and ought to control the ambition of the distressed mind."

Whose is the shout we hear, the angry cry of protest at these words? Whose else could it be but the outraged spirit of William Blake, in whose existence we all now participate? The great offended voice is raised to assert the power of the artist's imagination to deny the reality of the primordial Might, or to challenge and

[9] *Santayana: The Later Years,* 1963.

overcome it, or to interpose between it and us a dream, which, perhaps in the degree that it terrifies, commands our assent and holds out the promise of freedom.

If that is indeed what ideally we expect the imagination of the artist to do, Hawthorne does not satisfy our expectation. Again and again, in what we judge to be his too limited faith in the imagination, he admits, even insists, that the world is there, that we are dependent upon it. His quick response to the non-rational, his lively awareness of the primitive and chthonic, of the dark roots of life, does not deflect the naturalistic and humanistic tendency of his mind. At his very most powerful he does not interpose his imagination between us and the world; however successfully he may project illusion, he must point beyond it to the irrefrangible solidity.

He feared what Santayana called "the ambition of the distressed mind" and before the primordial Might he maintained an attitude of almost studied modesty, we might say of childlikeness when we remember what irony and malice he was capable of attributing to a child. Like a child, he takes liberties and plays tricks; he amuses himself and entertains us; he takes somber moral principles and makes them into toys—we have but to give to the idea of play the consideration it deserves to see that Henry James's description of his activity is not so deficient in justice as it first seems. Of his playfulness the ambivalence and ambiguity which are so often noted of him are essential aspects. But his ambivalence and ambiguity do not, I think, bring him close to Kafka's mute, riddling power—through them, rather, he approaches to Montaigne's *"Que sais-je?"*, the ironic childlike question, the question which conscious or calculated modesty asks, out of which all the questions come.

It is questions which Hawthorne leaves us with. It is, really, not at all clear why Young Goodman Brown must live out his life in sullenness because he refuses to sign the Devil's pact; nor is it clear why Robin must join the violent mob in laughter at his kinsman before he is his own master, and indeed it is not clear why being his own master is a wholly admirable condition. And when we consult ourselves for answers, we become aware of our dependence upon that part of the "efficacious but largely unfathomed background of human experience" which lies very close at hand, within our very selves, and which reminds us of our dependence upon its further reaches.

And in the degree that he does not dominate us, Hawthorne cannot wholly gratify us, moderns that we are. He is an exquisite artist, yet he suggests to us the limitations of art, and thus points to the stubborn core of actuality that is not to be overcome, and seems to say that the transaction between it and us is after all an unmediated one. And by his ambiguities and ambivalences he seems to imply that we—each one of us alone—must make our investigations and our terms as best we may. He has no great tyrant-dream in which we can take refuge, he leaves us face to face with the ultimately unmodifiable world, of which our undifferentiated human nature is a part. He does not even permit us what seems a complete view of the desperateness of our situation—nothing complete, nothing ultimate.

No, it is not gratifying. Yet if we tell the truth about our experience of Hawthorne, some of us will say that as we read him—or at moments as we read him—we have a sensation of having been set at liberty. It is not an entirely comfortable condition. We find ourselves at a loss and uncertain when we are in the charge of an artist so little concerned to impose upon us the structure of his imagination. We look for a more coercive will, and are insecure in its lack. Yet perhaps we feel, too, an impulse of exhilaration charging through our art-saturated minds, a new pleasure in being led carelessly or playfully to one or another dangerous place and being left alone to look at the danger in our own way. The pleasure cannot last long— probably more is needed in the life around us before such independent confrontations of our dependence will seem natural to us, and a kind of joy. Our judgment of Hawthorne may have to be that he is not for us today, and perhaps not even tomorrow. He is, in Nietzsche's phrase, one of the spirits of yesterday—and the day after tomorrow.

The Two Environments:
Reflections on
the Study of English

ALMOST a hundred years ago, nine notable teaching scholars undertook to examine the theory and practice of upper-class education in England. They were all distinguished by their learning in the classical languages and by their devotion to the ancient literatures, but most of them brought into question the predominant place that the study of Greek and Latin held in the public-school curriculum, to the exclusion of other subjects that seemed appropriate to the circumstances of the modern world. Their speculations and recommendations, edited by F. W. Farrar, were published as *Essays on a Liberal Education,* and the book is remembered, at least by people concerned with the theory of education, as a landmark in the development of modern schooling. Adamson, the historian of English education, speaks of it as "one of the earliest works to assert the possibility of a modern humanism, the possibility of extracting from modern literature much which was commonly thought to be derivable from a study of Greek and Latin alone."

In the making of this assertion, one of the essays, that by Henry Sidgwick, was especially cogent in its criticism of the hegemony of the two classical languages and in its proposal that, for most pupils, the study of Greek be replaced by the study of English. His argument proceeded on moral and political grounds, his chief point being that both in the private life and in the social life more enlightenment and sensibility were needed than the prevailing curriculum supplied. He said: "If so many of our expensively educated youth regard athletic sports as the one conceivable mode of enjoying leisure: if so many professional persons confine their extra-professional reading to the newspapers and novels: if the middle-class Englishman (as he is continually told) is narrow, unrefined, conventional, ignorant of what is really good and really evil in human life; if (as an uncompromising writer says) 'he is the tool of bigotry, the echo of stereotyped opinions, the victim of class prejudices, the great stumbling-block in the way of a general diffusion of a high cultivation in this country'—it is not because these persons have had a literary education which their 'invincible brutality' has rendered inefficacious: it is because the education has not been (to them) literary: in their study of Greek and Latin their minds have been simply put through various unmeaning linguistic exercises." And Sidgwick went on: "But the time seems to have come for us to discern and repair this natural mistake. Let us demand . . . that all boys, whatever their special bent and destination, be really taught literature: so that, as far as possible, they may learn to enjoy intelligently poetry and eloquence; that their interest in history may be awakened, stimulated and guided; that their views and sympathies may be enlarged and expanded by apprehending noble, subtle, and profound thoughts, refined and lofty feelings: that some comprehension of the various development of human nature may ever after abide with them, the source and essence of a truly humanizing culture. Thus in the prosecution of their special study or function, while their energy will be even stimulated, their views and aims will be more intelligent, more central; and therefore their work, if less absorbing, not less effective."

The year was 1867, the year of the Second Reform Bill, which virtually established the principle of political democracy in England and made plain how much of the old way of doing things would have to be given up. This was the year of the publication of *Culture and Anarchy,* in which, to a middle class "besotted with business," Matthew Arnold proposed as a means of salvation, as a means, indeed, of survival, the knowledge of the best that has been thought and said in the world. The terms of Arnold's conception of what literature might do for the health of the state are not exactly the same as Sidgwick's, but the two are much in accord; taken together, they constitute the rationale of our own modern theory of general education and they provide what is probably the strongest of all justifications that can be offered for making English literature a school or university subject.

Certain parts of the enterprise of education need little or no theoretical justification. Science is nowadays justified out of hand, if only by its connection with technology. Scarcely more is required to be said on behalf of the social and political sciences; their practical value is acknowledged, and it is obvious that they provide training for certain professions: from history, economics, sociology, come historians, economists, and sociologists, or civil servants for whom the social studies are of use. But the study of literature is not justified by practical and professional considerations. Those of us who teach the subject may be proud of our students who themselves go on to teach it, but we do not justify our profession by its powers of self-perpetuation. Nor would we are try to establish our credit in society by pointing to the poets and novelists who are produced by our teaching. Our rationalization must be wider: it must include the aims of education in its largest sense, or, as we say, its real sense. We must make reference to what in America we call—or used to call until we got sick of the phrase—the whole man. Other subjects also contribute to the making of the whole man—the study of music and the plastic arts, history, mathematics, science, and philosophy. But the study of literature has traditionally been felt to have a unique effectiveness in opening the mind and illuminating it, in purging the mind of prejudices and received ideas, in making the mind free and active. The classic defense of literary study holds that, from the effect which the study of literature has upon the private sentiments of a student, there results, or can be made to result, an improvement in the intelligence, and especially the intelligence as it touches the moral life.

This classic defense of literary study, the justification that was offered by Sidgwick and somewhat less explicitly by Arnold, has been, it would seem, of great efficacy. The profession of "English" teaching has established itself in the schools and even more impressively in the universities, and has become an important element in the intellectual life of England and America.[1] In America at least, the study of English has come to be thought of as the most usual and the most natural preparation for taking one's place in the intellectual life of the nation. Indeed, when we speak of "the intellectual," we are likely to have chiefly in mind the literary intellectual, the product of an English department. Less committed to method and to fact than the philosopher or the social scientist, licensed in emotion and intuition by the tradition of the subject he has studied, he ranges freely and directs his arguments to man-in-general. It is he who shows the most indignant face in moral and cultural dispute and who is most apt to assume that the intellectual life is dramatic.

In the development of the academic study of English there were two important stages. When it became plain that there was an anomaly in excluding from the university the study of the great literature of the mother-tongue, the discipline that was at last instituted occupied itself chiefly with the historical or "scientific" aspects of the subject. But this ascendancy of a scholarship which seemed far from humanistic was not permitted to last. About four decades ago the partisans of criticism began to wage war upon it. They

---

[1] I put "English" between quotation marks in order to be able to include both the English and the American situations in my purview. In England, if I understand the situation correctly, an English faculty or department confines its activity to English literature; in America an English department concerns itself not only with English but also with American literature and even with foreign literature in translation.

thought of themselves as isolated and outmatched and they regarded their subject, which was literature considered for its own sake and on its own terms and understood as having an influence on the feelings and actions of men in daily life, as undervalued and oppressed. The day of their heroism and pathos has passed and the brave small band with its guerrilla tactics and bold improvisations is now a proud profession. In America, even ten years ago, an English department had to search out recruits who had lively literary intelligences and at the same time a solid bottom of learning; now a department chooses with difficulty among the gifted critical minds which present themselves. Very likely a similar situation obtains in England.

If we look for the *mystique* from which the English-teaching profession drew its strength, we can scarcely fail to find it in the moral justification that was provided by Sidgwick and Arnold. The American whole-man theory assumes that the students' first concerns are practical. It may be that this assumption cannot nowadays be made with as much confidence and simplicity as once was possible, yet of course it may still be reasonably supposed that what Sidgwick calls "work" and Arnold calls "business" will occupy most university graduates and that a chief reason for their being in college is to prepare themselves for a life of work or business. We then say that we will not let them depart the university until they have submitted to certain humanizing and liberalizing disciplines, among which literature is pre-eminent. The English system of undergraduate education is very different from the American, but the justification of the study of literature is much the same in the two countries. In *The Muse Unchained,* an account of the development of the English School at Cambridge, Professor Tillyard, having remarked that the three Firsts in the School in a certain year did not pursue the study further, comforts himself with the thought that, after all, the purpose of studying English is not to "make dons but to construct people." If one undertakes the making of whole men or the construction of people, one does indeed have in mind the private lives of the men who are made whole or of the people who are constructed; but one's intention is also of a public kind which has ultimately to do with the state and with the quality of the persons who shall control the state, or at least with the quality of persons who shall criticize the state and make demands on it. This highly moralized intention, this public justification of the study of literature, was of course at the heart of the program put forward by the rebellious, the humanistic, the critical party of the English-teaching profession. Its having been made eloquently explicit by Sidgwick in part explains the special admiration in which he is held by Dr. and Mrs. Leavis. *Scrutiny* was not the whole of the insurgent movement of English teaching and with *Scrutiny* we all have had our quarrels, but we respect it and are grateful to it, and it was undeniably central to the critical movement. Without being overtly political, it undertook to construct people whose quality of intelligence, derived from literary study or refined by it, would ultimately affect the condition of society in certain good ways.

But now it must be a question whether the classic justification of the study of literature still has force. It evolved in circumstances in which one could attribute to literature a function which it may no longer have. Sidgwick and Arnold were thinking of a population of heavy minds dully gratified by the possession of heavy things. Not for nothing did Arnold in his lectures on Homer extol the virtues of clearness and rapidity—he wanted them for the English middle classes who, as he felt, existed in a state of sodden immobility. Sidgwick, too, was asking in effect for an increase in sensibility through literature, for a greater degree of emotional vivacity. Both men addressed themselves to a society sunk in material possession, in pride and self-satisfaction, in dogmatic religious belief, or, worse, habitual half-belief. Neither man foresaw the modern mobility, the contemporary suffusion of mind by ideas of a benign, enlightened, moralized, liberal kind. Neither foresaw the contemporary diffusion of artistic culture and its simulacra, a society drenched with art and with newspaper gossip about the arts. To the small band of pioneers who had to struggle for the establishment of the humanistic study of English in the universities, the old moral line was manifestly appropriate. These people might still have said, echoing Arnold, that the future of literature was immense. By this they would have meant that literature had yet to bring its moral influence to bear upon society. But we would seem to have arrived at the future. It is the present of literature that is immense, brought to its heroic proportions by social changes of which Arnold and Sidgwick could have no presentiment. Who in their day or even in the days that Professor Tillyard memorializes could have supposed that a time would come when a serious critic could possibly begin his discourse on literary education as Mr. Graham Hough begins his, with a description of the high place that literature holds in contemporary life, a place that can be thought of—this is Mr. Hough's point—as actually too high?[2]

No illusions need attend our awareness of this new state of affairs. It is clear that the whole of the British and American population has not fallen suddenly under the beneficent sway of literature. The influence and authority of literature extend to no more than certain sub-groups of the middle class. But these groups are considerable in size and they have great weight in our cultural life. It is they who pose the questions to the English-teaching profession, for they are to be found in great numbers among the new undergraduate population and in increasing and disproportionate numbers as candidates for degrees in English.

If the English faculties could suppose that the students were moved by a desire to understand the nature of literature and the history of the variations of its nature, and if they knew the students to be cheerfully devoted to the whole range of English literature from, say, Langland and Chaucer to, say, Gerard Manley Hopkins, this influx into English studies might seem to be a curious phenomenon but benign. What makes the troubled heart of the matter is the belief that the new undergraduates are characteristically

[2] *The Dream and the Task: Literature and Morals in the Culture of Today*, 1963.

drawn to modern literature and that, indeed, their appetite for the modern is not to be appeased by such figures as Yeats and Eliot, whose stature, complexity, and Victorian birth-dates offer the teacher a measure of reassurance—more and more the students press toward the contemporary and insist upon its being given pride of place in the curriculum. The stubbornness of faculties is magnificent, but the force of student preference, if it continues long enough, is irresistible, and one cannot help believing that the day will soon come in England as it has in America when one English faculty after another will say in effect what the Duke of Cambridge said upon his retirement from the Army after a career in which he had opposed all efforts of reform: "Gentlemen, there have been great changes in my time, great changes. But I can say this. Every change has been made at the right time, and the right time is when you cannot help it."

I have elsewhere[3] expressed a judgment on the American practice in the teaching of modern and even contemporary literature which is at least ambivalent, and I am far from urging now that it be emulated in England. And I do not in fact believe that it is likely to be emulated in the very near future. The American theory of undergraduate education being what it is, we can permit ourselves a considerable latitude in our selection of the books we teach. In some quarters the feeling exists that almost any involvement with literature is better than none. There are even those who would say that J. D. Salinger or Arthur Miller does more than Milton can to convey to the students what Sidgwick calls, "noble, subtle, and profound thoughts, refined and lofty feelings," and to give them some comprehension of "the varied development of human nature." In England, where undergraduate specialization still prevails, there is the expectable emphasis on an historical tradition. The American system, conceiving of literature as a necessary element, but only an element, in a general university education, supposes that enough has been done if the sensibility of the undergraduate has been engaged,

[3] See the essay, "On the Teaching of Modern Literature."

although of course a great deal more than this is often accomplished. In England, the study of English may be, for those students who choose it, the whole of their university training, and its intellectual benefit is presumed to come through a *mastery* of the subject. This is a circumstance that will make the English acceptance of the modern relatively slow. And in general, as compared with America, England is not a culturally mobile nation. The process which Mr. Harold Rosenberg has described, in which American public intellectual agencies, such as museums, university art departments, and professional publications can bring about the quick acceptance of new kinds of painting and not only "make into art what is now not art" but also unmake what is now art—this process does not operate so freely in England. The response of England to extreme ideologies in art is likely to be somewhat reluctant; cultural choices do not seem so momentous as they do in America. Among the American intellectual classes strong feeling is directed to the issues of culture, for which the issues of politics are often but a mask. The English still allocate most of their fund of partisan emotion to politics, perhaps led to do so by their residual feelings about social class.

But, as I have said, the English distribution of emotion is likely to change—it is probable that more and more response will be made to the stimuli offered by the contemporary culture, and the English faculties of the English universities will have to take account of this increased sensitivity. Indeed, the change is already enough apparent to have provoked adverse editorial comment from the *Times Literary Supplement*. It was said of the students who now crowd the English departments of the universities that they choose English out of lack of intellectual stamina, believing it to be an easy subject, and that they prefer modern to traditional writers because their imaginations are undeveloped. The article was entitled "Without It" and thus made reference to the faded but perhaps still viable phrase "with it," meaning to be aware of and on easy terms with what is authoritative in the cultural life, especially in the arts as they suggest styles of personality: ultimately the phrase celebrates the ability to receive accurately the message of the *Zeitgeist*. The editorial comment intended chiefly to suggest that the students' preferences were modish and faddish. Perhaps so; but it is necessary to recognize the part a mode or a fad may play in the history of culture. The English middle classes of the sixteenth and seventeenth centuries fell prey to a fad of Bible-reading and theological radicalism. It is hard for us to imagine how these Puritan predilections could once have impassioned many minds, but before they passed beyond our comprehension, they changed the social and cultural fabric of England and helped create the social and cultural fabric of America.

The analogy is not gratuitous. It has been said by many, myself among them, that literature, modern literature in particular, now stands virtually in the place of religion and may even be thought of as itself a religion. Mr. Hough puts it that literature is now required to "provide the foundations of feeling, conduct and belief for those who have no other source of supply." And of this literary religion or quasi-religion Mr. Hough says that it is "without a system, without an ethic, without a creed." With this I cannot entirely agree. If literature, or art in general, has become a religion, it may be difficult to trace out its "system" and to formulate its "creed," but its ethic is by no means obscure.

Indeed, when we try to understand the impulse that leads so many students to make their way into the English departments of the universities, we may well conclude that it is in large part a moral impulse. I speak only from my experience of American students, but I am confident that it is no less true of students in England that an involvement with modern literature goes with an insistent—perhaps it is to be called a nagging—concern with morality. Confronted by the high moral sensitivity of his students, the teacher of English might well feel that he is deprived of one function of his profession. He can no longer suppose that his pupils' views and sympathies need to be enlarged and expanded (as Sidgwick put it) by instruction in literature. He is not, to be sure, teaching a new race of young moral geniuses, but neither is he rescuing his pupils from a social situation which fosters an "invincible brutality." Their very eager-ness to study literature precludes such a possibility. It is a pre-eminent enterprise of our culture to produce the judgment of "what is really good and really evil in human life." The teacher can no longer flatter himself that this work is peculiarly his.

But if we speak of the students' concern with what is really good and really evil in human life, we must not conclude that this is a concern with morality in the traditional sense of the word, certainly not in the sense in which it was likely to be used in the nineteenth century. Sidgwick, whose most memorable book is his work on ethics, tells us in an autobiographical memoir that in his ethical theory he began as an adherent of John Stuart Mill. For a consider-able time he saw no inconsistency between the two elements of Mill's system, the impulse of a man to seek his own happiness and his less overt impulse to seek the happiness of all. Sidgwick was attracted to both elements, to the former because of its "frank natu-ralism," to the latter because of its inspiring dictate of readiness for "absolute self-sacrifice." Eventually he saw that the two impulses, so far from being in harmony, made a dilemma. He thereupon set himself to "examine methodically the relation of Interest and Duty." How he resolved the dilemma to his own satisfaction need not concern us: I recall the episode in his intellectual life only to suggest how alien to us is what was so natural to Sidgwick, the perception of an ethical dilemma and the methodical examination of it. This old way of conceiving of the moral life still has a degree of meaning for us. We *understand* it. We can, for example, still take pleasure in the novelist who, perhaps more fully than any other, represents the old ethical mode, and we consider that Henry James is indeed being praised when he is called "the historian of fine consciences." But what novelist of our day might we celebrate with that phrase? Mr. Raymond Williams has said that in our time a "civilized and espe-cially a literate man" is overtaken by hysterical anxiety when he is spoken to in moral terms. This is certainly not to say that the civilized literate man of our time has no moral consciousness. But his—our—moral consciousness is very different from that exemplified by Sidgwick. So far from taking explicit account of ethical dilemmas, we believe that ethical dilemmas, confrontations of opposing principles of conduct, do not—because they should not, because they need not—exist.

The negation does not leave the modern morality without positive intention. Far from it; its intention is very positive indeed and may perhaps best be defined in the phrase that Yeats once used to explain the intention of magic. "The ultimate object of magic in all ages," Yeats said, "was, and is, to obtain control of the sources of life." By "the sources of life" Yeats meant, we may suppose, not only what supports existence but what yields to man the fullness, freedom, and potency of life he desires. The intention of obtaining control of the sources of life has always been part of the purpose of both literature and religion. And it has not been alien from the purpose of morality, even when morality has seemed to be most repressive. But the intention has never so fully governed literature as it does today. And most certainly it has never been in such absolute command of morality as it now is. If Sidgwick's particular dilemma, the contradiction between Interest and Duty, no longer engages us, I think we can say that this is because the modern morality, in its powerful imagination of the sources of life and the need to obtain control over them, denies the contradiction between Interest and Duty. Typically in our culture, when a person of good will thinks of the control of the sources of life, he conceives of it as assuring the happiness both of the individual and of the generality of mankind. He assumes that there is a continuity between what he desires for himself and what he desires for others—what he wants for himself in the way of fullness, freedom, and potency is the paradigm of what he wants for others; what he wants for others he thinks of as the guarantee of the fullness, freedom, and potency he wants for himself.

Thus described, the moral temper of our time might well seem to deserve great praise and to give us ground for self-congratulation. Concerned as it is with the Greatest Happiness of the Greatest

Number, it yet does not feel the need to undergo examination by the Utilitarian rationality that Sidgwick exemplifies. We might almost believe that we had come close to that stage in the development of mankind which Schiller predicted and longed for, in which the moral life is no longer problematical and painful, in which, indeed, it does not really exist—perhaps at last we are on the way to being released from the old bondage to Necessity and have actually got one foot into the realm of Freedom, where the faculty of conscientious reason is no longer needed. A true relation to the sources of life does not refer to rational criteria; it is expressed not in doctrine, not in systems, ethics, and creeds, but in manner and style. We know whether or not a person is in touch with the sources of life not by what he says, by its doctrinal correctness, but by the way he says it, by the tone of his voice, the look in his eye, by his manner and style. So too with a society: we know if it is really in touch with the sources of life not by its mere practical arrangements but by the style of life that it fosters—in short, by its *culture,* which we judge as a whole, rather as if it were a work of art.

The criterion of style, the examination of life by aesthetic categories, yields judgments of a subtle and profound kind, of compelling force. Such judgments are the stuff of the great classic literature of the modern period. Yeats and Eliot, Lawrence and Joyce, each in his own way, have instructed us how to make these judgments for ourselves, teaching us that there can be nothing within that passeth show, that whatever is within of grace or lack of grace will manifest itself in the timbre of the voice, the rhythm of the speech, in how the foot meets the ground, in the feel of the chosen cloth, in the fashion of the house inhabited. By such things we learn to know our neighbors; they yield a knowledge that transcends the knowledge of mere actions. They make the ground for a kind of judgment more searching and exigent than that of the old morality of the deed, a judgment that is rather cruel, really, but fascinating; it promises not only a new kind of truth but a new kind of power, very exciting.

It is notoriously difficult to dispute about style in a coherent rational way. But it is not difficult to dispute about style in *some* way. And when style is regarded as an index to morality, as showing what the relation of someone or something is to the sources of life, the passions of the dispute will be very intense. The extraordinary anger that Dr. Leavis directed against C. P. Snow a few years ago is to be accounted for by the latter's having dared to conjure the sources of life in a style that Dr. Leavis believed wrong. In Dr. Leavis's view, it was not so much that his antagonist held mistaken opinions or subscribed to wrong doctrines, the imputed error being demonstrable by reason, it was rather that his magic was of the wrong kind, his medicines of bad omen: Lord Snow's incantations were in a style that Dr. Leavis held to be inadmissible.

This famous instance of stylistic polemic is less typical of the critical practice of England than of America, where it is the mark of the culturally sensitive critic to concentrate upon manner and tone and to express his judgment upon these in a mode that reaches, as it is intended to reach, the point of personal inculpation. But it is probable that the idiom of "cultural," as opposed to intellectual, debate will soon be adopted by the English too. The intense concern with questions of style, the assumption that style is an effectual means of commanding the highest degree of fullness, freedom, and potency of life, is consonant with certain aspects of modern societies. It must now be one of the commonplaces of sociology that, less in England than in America, but increasingly in England (as well as in certain European countries), the economy itself is deeply involved with matters of style and with the conditions of the spirit or psyche. Our commodities are not only mere *things* but states of mind: joy, freedom, self-definition, self-esteem. One industry after another is benefited by our ever-growing need to choose a fashion of dress, or décor, or locomotion which will serve to signalize some spiritual or psychic grace. Advertising joins forces with literature in agitating the question of who one is, of what kind of person one should want to be, a choice in which one's possessions and appearance, one's tastes, are as important as one's feelings and behavior. It was D. H.

Lawrence who said that not until men once again got themselves up in tight red hose and short jerkins that showed the buttocks would they come into a right relation with the sources of life. It was Yeats who asserted the peculiar moral authenticity of gray Connemara cloth.

The impulse to choose, define, and indicate what kind of person one is can scarcely be thought new, and we shall regard it more charitably if we are aware of how deeply rooted it is in human nature, and how we love the charm of spirit it can often display. What *is* new is the moralizing attitude which now supports this impulse, and the boldness with which it is offered as a principle of social organization; increasingly people find it possible to escape from the old categories of class and to come together in categories of taste. Style takes its unabashed place, as I have tried to suggest, in the process of intellect.

Both Sidgwick and Arnold had of course asserted that the study of literature eventually bears upon the principles of social organization and upon the right management of the processes of the intellect. At the heart of the English-teaching profession's sense of its function there has long stood Arnold's famous statement, battered but indestructible, that literature is a criticism of life—the profession has never been content to say that its purpose was to develop the aesthetic response to literature; the study of literature was always meant to contribute to the power of the critical intelligence, and the "life" upon which the critical intelligence was to be directed was the social life, or, what for the purposes of the profession was the same thing, the cultural life, the anomalies and inequities of the one, the vulgarities and deficiencies of the other. Here is a recent statement of the aims of English teaching which seems to me to represent the tradition in a sufficiently accurate way though its expression is unhappy: "What the intelligent citizen dissatisfied with the cultural state of his society must work for is, first, mere awareness of the position, and then a habit of discrimination in reacting to the present, an attempt to carry forward into the future what is valuable in the past, a readiness to single out the rare good in the present and be ready to proclaim it. Inevitably also he will believe in the power of education as a counter to the trivializing forces of our society. Hence . . . education becomes what George Sampson had thought it to be in his *English for the English* in 1922: an active unfitting of the pupil to his future environment. And Sampson foresaw the same means: education through the vernacular language and its literature."[4]

Most people concerned with literary education will be moved to give this statement their assent. It represents, I believe, and not least in its earnestness, the long-established habit of the profession's thought. Yet to assent to it now is not, we must see, what it would have been to assent to it in 1922—it is by no means the same thing to work now for "an active unfitting of the pupil to his future environment" as when George Sampson made his formulation. In most respects the society of 1922 was probably closer to that of 1867 than to that of the present decade. In either of the earlier times, to unfit the pupil to his future environment would have been to detach him from the prejudices and presuppositions—from the "values"—of a single prepotent cultural environment, to expect that he would show himself to be a person of firm character and independent mind, committed to such fortitude as is needed if someone is to take up a position outside the cultural environment in which he was reared. We cannot nowadays believe that, in the interests of his best development, we are separating a student from so much or putting him to anything like so severe a test. He is not being sent into the wilderness, alone, a banished man; we can scarcely fail to know that there stands ready to receive him another "environment" in which he is pretty sure to be tolerably comfortable, an environment that is organized and that has its own roots in the general economy.

The fact is that the student today is at liberty to choose between two cultural environments. One of them can no doubt be described in terms not unlike those that Sidgwick and Arnold used of the

---

[4] Michael Black, "The Third Realm," *The Use of English*, Volume XV, Number 4, Summer 1964, page 281.

class-bound England of a century ago—it is perhaps less proud and less self-praising, but we can take it to be Philistine and dull, satisfied with its unexamined, unpromising beliefs. The other environment defines itself by its difference from and its antagonism to the first, by its commitment to the "sources of life," by its adherence to the imagination of fullness, freedom, and potency of life, and to what goes with this imagination, the concern with moralized taste and with the styles which indicate that one has successfully gained control of the sources of life or which are themselves a means of gaining that control.

As thus described, the second environment would seem to be the more appealing of the two. It is here that art resides, and where art is, life is—surely that is true? But as we watch the development of the second cultural environment, we become less and less certain that it is entirely free of the traits that we reprobate in the first, which may have led us to wish to unfit our students for it. This second environment must always have *some* ethical or spiritual advantage over the first, if only because, even though its influence and its personnel do indeed grow apace, it will never have the actual rule of the world; if its personnel sometimes dreams of rule, it yet knows that it would become bored by the dreary routine that rulers must submit to: the blame for the ugly actualities of rule will therefore always rest on Philistine shoulders. But as our students find it ever easier to take their places in the second cultural environment, as they are ever surer of finding comfort and companions in it, we have to see that it shows the essential traits of any cultural environment: firm presuppositions, received ideas, approved attitudes, and a system of rewards and punishments. The student who decides to enter this second environment, if he considers it from the distance of some provincial city or town, or of a family strong in whatever class feelings it may have, may understandably take his steps toward it in a dramatic mood, in the belief that he ventures into the uncharted fearsome territory of freedom. In point of fact, as his teachers must know if they have any right sense of our life at the present time, he is joining one of the two established cultural parties. If the one he has chosen is in the minority, the party of opposition, this has its recognized advantages.

The situation is not necessarily to be deplored. It must inevitably attract a degree of wryness but this is only because the second environment still finds it to its purpose to call upon a pathos which is no longer appropriate to its size and strength. But considered objectively, by a cultural historian of the future or a sociologist of the present, the situation of the two environments might be thought of as a wise and prudent way of compounding the differences that are natural to a great national society. Many teachers of English might incline to take this view. They might feel that what is referred to in Sidgwick's essay as "a general diffusion of a high cultivation" is guaranteed by the existence of this second environment, that a sufficient number of their students prove the development of their intelligences by moving from the old environment to the new, and that as teachers they were doing all that might be done if they facilitated the emigration.

But some teachers will not be content to see things so. If they believe that education has the power (and duty) to act as "a counter to the trivializing forces of our society," they may feel that the teaching of literature is no longer able to bring that power to bear. If they are aware of the existence of the two environments, they may even be disposed to think that in the very structure of the second there exists a trivializing force. And although these teachers may feel this the more in the degree that the curriculum responds to the demand, made in the interests of "relevance" and "immediacy," that it deal with modern literature, they will not easily recognize this connection or, recognizing it, they will be puzzled to account for it if they are themselves young or relatively young people who have responded strongly to the great classic literature of modern times. The literature itself is not trivial. But there has grown out of this literature, or around it, a cultural environment which might well lead some serious teachers to think twice before undertaking to prepare their students to enter it.

What they discern and are dismayed by is perhaps suggested by

Saul Bellow in the remarks he made upon the occasion of a recent award to his latest novel, *Herzog*. In his brief speech of acceptance Mr. Bellow made fully explicit and polemical a view of modern literature that had already found expression in his novel. With considerable severity he remarked upon a long-established assumption of the "advanced" part of our culture, that man is most accurately and significantly represented as being in a state of "alienation," that the extent of a writer's own alienation is a first measure of his interest and importance. And Mr. Bellow referred to the judgment which naturally goes along with the doctrine of alienation, that "modern society is frightful, brutal, hostile to whatever is pure in the human spirit, a waste land and a horror." The adversary position that Mr. Bellow took toward the prevailing dark view of the human condition has of course been taken many times before, but perhaps never by anyone so fully accredited to the literary public as Mr. Bellow is, so reassuringly *modern,* so remote from Philistinism.

One could wish that Mr. Bellow had chosen a different occasion for a statement which offered so violent an affront to a view which, with the passing of time, has acquired great authority, even sacrosanctity. His position deserves a more fully developed examination than Mr. Bellow gave it; it would have been better had he invited not merely the assent of a public gathering but the considered discourse of those colleagues to whom his remarks are of most immediate concern. But surely Mr. Bellow's statement that the modern novel is losing its force and that it will become "truly irrelevant" unless the novelists begin to *think* and to "make a clear estimate of our situation" brings into open debate an idea which has for too long had for us a virtually totemistic power. I use the word *totemistic* advisedly, having in mind the "odd totems" which Professor Lévi-Strauss tells us are to be found in Australia: "laughing, various illnesses, vomiting, and a corpse."[5]

Mr. Bellow does not quite say that the dark view of the modern condition is false, only that "it is one of the traditions on which literature has lived uncritically." Now, in general, there is nothing

[5] *Totemism*, 1963, page 63.

wrong in literature living on a tradition which it accepts uncritically—this would seem to be part of the ecology of the literary process as we know it through the ages. But our modern fiction undertakes consciously to perform acts of criticism. Its doctrine of alienation is an act of criticism. And as Mr. Bellow correctly points out, this doctrine of our novelists is accepted uncritically even by our critics. ". . . The critics must share the blame," Mr. Bellow says. "They too have failed to describe the situation. Literature has for several generations been its own source, its own province, has lived upon its own traditions, and accepted a romantic separation or estrangement from the common world. This estrangement, though it has produced some masterpieces, has by now enfeebled literature." This inculpation of the critics is particularly to our present point. One of the commonplaces of the history of modern literature is the brilliant energy of our criticism. Yet if we judge the matter closely, after we have given criticism the praise that is surely its due, we must go on to say that its achievement has been, after all, of an elementary sort. It has taught us how to read certain books; it has not taught us how to engage them. Modern literature (it need scarcely be said again) is directed toward moral and spiritual renovation; its subject is damnation and salvation. It is a literature of doctrine which, although often concealed, is very aggressive. The occasions are few when criticism has met this doctrine on its own fierce terms. Of modern criticism it can be said that it has instructed us in an intelligent passivity before the beneficent aggression of literature. Attributing to literature virtually angelic powers, it has passed the word to the readers of literature that the one thing you do not do when you meet an angel is wrestle with him.

If this can be said of criticism in general, how much more can it be said of that special form of criticism which is teaching. The teacher's first job is to lead his students to accept what is odd and to understand what is difficult in a work. Often there is no time to do more than this. Often a full comprehension of the work lies beyond the powers of the student even though these powers may be sufficient for a first understanding of it. Often, because he has had to give so much energy to its comprehension and exposition, the teacher develops a vested interest in the work and has not the heart to put it to the doctrinal question.[6] These circumstances are to be understood and forgiven, but perhaps one reason why the modern relation to literature is open to the charge of triviality is that it begins for so many readers in an inadequate classroom training.

And if we think of Mr. Bellow's speech not primarily in its substance, but only as an event, and if we then contemplate the kind of response it evokes, we have perhaps a fair index to the character of what I have been calling the second environment. By now, of course, the speech has become part of the *mythos* of that environment. Everyone has been a little scandalized, some have been pleased and relieved by it, others angered and embittered. What we have not yet had is any effort to consider in a consequential way whether what was said was right or wrong, in how far right, in how far wrong, why right and why wrong. It has its chief existence in the realm of gossip, that great new transcendent gossip of the second environment, where it is used as evidence of the quality of being, the grace or lack of grace, of the speaker and of those who think it right and of those who think it wrong.

If this is indeed our situation, then those few teachers I have been imagining, who do not think that preparing their students for entrance into the second environment is enough to do for them in the way of education, may one day have to question whether in our culture the study of literature is any longer a suitable means for developing and refining the intelligence. The theory of literary education as it was first formulated supposed that literature carried the self beyond the culture, that it induced or allowed the self to detach itself from its bondage to the idols of the Marketplace, the Tribe, the Theatre, and even of the Cave. Perhaps literature was once able to do this, or something near enough to it to satisfy the theory. But

---

[6] I leave out of account the theory, which is influential in academic life but not dominant, that questions of doctrine are wholly irrelevant to literary study.

now we must ask whether this old intention has not been inverted, and whether literature does not, in fact, set up the old idols in new forms of its own contrivance.

There is a passage in Keats's letters which, when it is read by anyone who has anything to do with literature, should make the earth shake, although it does not; which should momently haunt our minds, although it does not. It is the passage in which Keats, having previously said that poetry is not so fine a thing as philosophy, ends with the phrase, ". . . an eagle is not so fine a thing as a truth." Considering the man who wrote it, it is an awesome utterance, in part because it appears to be a betrayal of the man's own life. But this was not the only occasion on which Keats reminded us that there is something more important than poetry; in fact, his ability to say this would seem to have been an essential part of his genius as a poet. "Though a quarrel in the streets is a thing to be hated," he wrote, "the energies displayed in it are fine; the commonest Man shows a grace in his quarrel—By a superior being our reasonings may take the same tone—though erroneous they may be fine—This is the very thing in which consists poetry; and if so it is not so fine a thing as philosophy—For the same reason that an eagle is not so fine a thing as a truth."

Bibliographical Note

"On the Teaching of Modern Literature" was first published (as "On the Modern Element in Modern Literature") in *Partisan Review*, January–February 1961.

The essay on Jane Austen's *Emma* was written as the introduction to the Riverside Edition of that novel (Boston: Houghton Mifflin Company, 1957). By permission of Houghton Mifflin Company it was also published in *Encounter*, June 1957.

"The Fate of Pleasure" was first published in *Partisan Review*, Summer 1963.

"Freud: Within and Beyond Culture" was delivered as The Freud Anniversary Lecture to the New York Psychoanalytical Society and the New York Psychoanalytical Institute in May 1955, under the title "Freud and the Crisis of Our Culture," and it was published under that title by Beacon Press (Boston, 1955). It has been somewhat revised from its first published form.

The essay on Isaac Babel was written as the introduction to *The Collected Stories of Isaac Babel* (New York: Criterion Books, Inc., 1955). By permission of Criterion Books, Inc., it was also published in *Commentary*, June 1955.

"A Comment on the Leavis-Snow Controversy" was first published in *Commentary*, June 1962.

"Hawthorne in Our Time" was written for *Hawthorne Centenary Essays* (Columbus: Ohio State University Press, 1964), where it was entitled "Our Hawthorne." By permission of Ohio State University Press it was also published in *Partisan Review*, Summer 1964.

"The Two Environments: Reflections on the Study of English" was read as The Henry Sidgwick Memorial Lecture at Newnham College, Cambridge University, on February 20, 1965. The present version is somewhat revised from the one that was published in *Encounter,* July 1965.